DATA ANALYTICS
ELEVATING INTERNAL AUDIT'S VALUE

Warren W. Stippich Jr., CIA, CPA, CRMA

Bradley J. Preber, CPA/CFF, CGMA, CFE, CCA

Grant Thornton

An instinct for growth™

The Institute of Internal Auditors
Research Foundation

The Institute of
Internal Auditors
Dallas Chapter

Published by The Institute of Internal Auditors Research Foundation
247 Maitland Avenue
Altamonte Springs, Florida 32701-4201

The Institute of Internal Auditors' (IIA's) International Professional Practices Framework (IPPF) comprises the full range of existing and developing practice guidance for the profession. The IPPF provides guidance to internal auditors globally and paves the way to world-class internal auditing.

The IIA and The IIARF work in partnership with researchers from around the globe who conduct valuable studies on critical issues affecting today's business world. Much of the content presented in their final reports is a result of IIARF-funded research and prepared as a service to The IIARF and the internal audit profession. Expressed opinions, interpretations, or points of view represent a consensus of the researchers and do not necessarily reflect or represent the official position or policies of The IIA or The IIARF.

"Grant Thornton" refers to Grant Thornton LLP, the U.S. member firm of Grant Thornton International Ltd (GTIL), and/or refers to the brand under which the GTIL member firms provide audit, tax and advisory services to their clients, as the context requires. GTIL and each of its member firms are separate legal entities and are not a worldwide partnership. GTIL does not provide services to clients. Services are delivered by the member firms in their respective countries. GTIL and its member firms are not agents of, and do not obligate, one another and are not liable for one another's acts or omissions. In the United States, visit grantthornton.com for details.

ISBN-13: 978-0-89413-964-2
20 19 18 17 16   1 2 3 4 5 6

CONTENTS

LIST OF EXHIBITS

FOREWORD

Gold symbolizes wealth, power, and status. Today, data is like the gold of the future, and everyone is rushing to stake a claim. Internal audit is no different as it seeks to make its own claim on this valuable asset. Mined using data analytics and refined into commercial assets, like gold bullion, data becomes the source of wealth, power, and status. It also becomes a road map that may help internal audit ensure it delivers tangible value to the organization.

Data analytics can elevate internal audit performance and create organizational value. However, there is no established path to capture the benefits of data analytics, in part because internal audit departments run the gamut in size and maturity. To understand this challenge and how the internal audit community is addressing it, Grant Thornton LLP partnered with The IIARF to conduct in-depth research into how internal audit departments use data analytics.

We developed this book with a few objectives in mind. First, we establish how internal audit departments currently use data analytics through surveys with members of The IIA and one-on-one interviews with many chief audit executives (CAEs), internal audit directors, and data analytics managers across the United States. Second, we provide internal audit leaders a better understanding of the data analytics strategies and tools available to enhance the function. Last, and most important, we present a structured framework that offers an option on how internal audit departments can more fully develop and integrate data analytics.

We would like to thank the CAEs, internal audit directors, and data analytics managers—and their broader teams—whose insights are integral to this book. Their willingness to share their successes, challenges, and aspirations has been of enormous value. This book would not have been possible without their contributions and we acknowledge each of them on the acknowledgments page. A special thank you to Mark Salamasick, executive director of audit at the University of Texas System, for his advice and guidance during this endeavor.

In many ways, this is a pivotal moment for internal audit. The coming years will see all facets of internal audit undergo a significant evolution due to advancements in technology and capitalization on the use of data. Even in the face of great change, there is cause for optimism. By making strategic investments now, internal audit departments have the potential to further enhance their value to organizations and stand ready for the challenges ahead. We hope this book will provide useful insights to help guide your data analytics journey.

Warren W. Stippich Jr.

Bradley J. Preber

ACKNOWLEDGMENTS

The IIARF would like to thank the Board of Trustees, the Committee of Research and Education Advisors (CREA) members, and staff for dedicating their talent and expertise to the project.

Steve Mar, CREA Review Team Lead

Karen Begelfer, CREA Member

Sezer Bozkus, CREA Member

Karin Hill, CREA Member

David Williams, CREA Member

The IIARF Board of Trustees

Bonnie Ulmer, Vice President, IIARF

Lillian McAnally, Managing Editor/Project Manager, IIARF

Lee Ann Campbell, Senior Publications Editor, IIARF

Deborah Poulalion, Data Analyst

The IIARF also would like to recognize the IIA–Dallas Chapter for its generous donation in sponsoring the project to advance the internal audit profession.

The Institute of
Internal Auditors
Dallas Chapter

We thank the following organizations and individuals for sharing their insight into how data analytics can maximize value for the internal audit community.

Ace Hardware
Tim Baker, Director of Audit Services

Advance Auto Parts
Tom Belt, Chief Audit Executive
Denise Stewart, Internal Audit Manager
Kevin Nicholson, Senior Internal Auditor

American Heart Association
Vickie Tesmer, Director of Audit and Consulting Services

AmerisourceBergen
Andrew Schmidt, Vice President and Director of Internal Audit

Baylor Scott & White Health
Monica Frazer, Vice President, Internal Audit

CF Industries
Mary Ann Tourney, Chief Audit Executive

Chevron Corporation
Mario Boffa, Group Manager of Corporate Audit
Jamie Dubray, IT Audit Client Manager
Angelin Butler, Data Resource Manager
Mark Ross, Audit Client Manager
Linda Ware, Data Business Analyst

Cleveland Clinic
Don Sinko, Chief Integrity Officer

Coca-Cola Bottling Co.
Ann Andreoli, Manager of Internal Control Services

DeVry University
Elizabeth Truelove McDermott, Vice President, Audit, Ethics & Compliance Services

Discover Financial Services
Jeff Song, Director of Internal Audit
Michael Nesler, Vice President, Internal Audit
Vesela Zlateva, Vice President, IT Audit

Duke University
Michael Somich, Executive Director of Internal Audits

Federal Signal Corporation
Mike Pryal, Vice President, Internal Audit

KeyBank
Elvis Kanlic, Senior Vice President, Data Analytics

Kimberly-Clark Corporation
Abe Paul, Global Director of Internal Audit

Lennox International
Charles Donnelly, Chief Audit Executive

Lowe's Companies
Lori Cairo, Chief Audit Executive
Clark Simmers, Corporate Audit Manager

Martin Marietta Materials
Cesar Perez, Vice President, Internal Audit

MoneyGram International
Manny Rosenfeld, Senior Vice President, Internal Audit

Och-Ziff Capital Management Group
Michael Rosenberg, Chief Audit Executive

Overhead Door Corporation
Marc Winandy, Audit Director

Packaging Corporation of America
Mark Pearson, Director of Internal Audit

Sherwin-Williams
John Hullibarger, Director, Corporate Audit
David Walther, IT Audit Manager

University of Maryland University College (UMUC)
Kathleen Sobieralski, Director of the Undergraduate Accounting Program

University of Texas System
Mike Peppers, Chief Audit Executive
Mark Salamasick, Executive Director of Audit
Dyan Hudson, Assistant Director, Specialty Audit Services

The professionals of Grant Thornton LLP dedicated considerable resources to research, interview, compile, and develop a book that would truly benefit the broader internal audit community. We make special acknowledgment of the following individuals.

NAME	TITLE	LOCATION
John Barnes	Partner	Baltimore, MD
Chris Bell	Principal	Houston, TX
Anthony Bohorquez	Senior Manager	Los Angeles, CA
Joseph Coniker	Principal	Raleigh, NC
Ronald Cote	Managing Director	Chicago, IL
Jim Culbreth	Director	Raleigh, NC
Scott Graham	Manager	Chicago, IL
Katherine Herrick	Manager	Boston, MA
Philip Higginbotham	Director	Dallas, TX
Bailey Jordan	Partner	Raleigh, NC
Paul Klein	Managing Director	Iselin, NJ
Fred Kohm	Partner	Philadelphia, PA
Alex Koltsov	Manager	Phoenix, AZ
Brian Lopez	Director	Los Angeles, CA
Bruce Orr	Director	Houston, TX
Matt Petrich	Senior Manager	Chicago, IL
Phil Quimby	Director	Alexandria, VA
Mike Rose	Partner	Philadelphia, PA
Priya Sarjoo	Principal	Dallas, TX
Paul Seckar	Senior Manager	Alexandria, VA
Evangeline Umali	Manager	Chicago, IL
Greg Wallig	Principal	Alexandria, VA
Skip Westfall	Managing Director	Houston, TX
Ben Wilner	Managing Director	Chicago, IL
Andy Wilson	Manager	Los Angeles, CA

ABOUT THE AUTHORS

Warren W. Stippich Jr., CIA, CPA, CRMA, is partner, national governance, risk and compliance practice leader, global co-leader of Grant Thornton's Business Risk Services. He has more than 25 years of experience working with multi-national, entrepreneurial, and high-growth public companies, including boards of directors and audit committees. He leads many Sarbanes-Oxley consulting and internal audit services for a wide array of publicly traded and private businesses with international operations. He has worked extensively with international internal audit, Sarbanes-Oxley, and business consulting assignments in Europe, Russia, China, India, Southeast Asia, Central and South America, and Canada.

Warren currently serves on The IIARF's Board of Trustees. He is also an advisory board member for the Department of Accountancy and board member of the College of Business Alumni Association at the University of Illinois at Urbana-Champaign.

Bradley J. Preber, CPA/CFF, CGMA, CFE, CCA, is national managing partner of Grant Thornton's Forensic and Valuation Services. He has more than 30 years of experience serving as a litigation consultant, expert witness, forensic accountant, and fraud investigator. He specializes in complex claims and events, with a particular emphasis on commercial disputes and fraud claims. Brad also serves on Grant Thornton's Partnership Board and was formerly the managing partner for the Desert Southwest offices.

Brad frequently speaks, writes, and teaches on leadership, accounting, and fraud-related matters. His book, *Financial Expert Witness Communication: A Practical Guide to Reporting and Testimony*, was recently published by John Wiley & Sons, Inc.

INTRODUCTION

Imagine an organization where the internal audit department has ready access to data from every department, business line, and function. An organization where internal auditors use intimate knowledge of the enterprise to continuously monitor activities and identify both risks and opportunities from entire populations of data. An organization where internal audit is a strategic partner with the C-Suite and key business process owners are trained and leveraged to be extensions of the internal audit team.

While these capabilities might seem like a next-generation fantasy for internal audit, this reality is right around the corner with the advent of data analytics—the process of gathering and examining data with the intention to use the results to facilitate an improved decision-making process. Arguably, no single group has greater potential to translate data analytics into organizational value than internal audit. However, the adoption of data analytics by internal auditors to date has largely been limited.

In the coming years, data analytics in internal audit will become widespread and mainstream. Internal audit professionals that hesitate to incorporate data analytics more fully into their operations will fall behind and risk becoming obsolete. The transformation will require a concerted effort to enhance people, process, and technology as the strategic drivers to realize the vision.

This book—the brainchild of The IIARF and Grant Thornton LLP—was developed to be a practical guide to help internal auditors understand, adopt, and successfully integrate data analytics into everyday workflows and long-term initiatives. The foundation for the book is based on surveys, interviews, and focus groups consisting of internal audit leadership and practitioners (see **sidebar, About the Research**).

Internal audit professionals will learn the necessary steps toward developing a plan to capitalize on data analytics technology and resources. The book begins with an overview of data analytics, along with basic terminology and its common usages. The second chapter offers a Data Analytics Framework to help with assessing current and future states. The framework consists of four steps:

1. Develop a vision.

2. Evaluate current capabilities.

3. Enhance people, process, and technology.

4. Implement, monitor, and evolve.

Chapters 3 through 6 examine each step of the Data Analytics Framework. Chapter 7 looks at the future of data analytics in internal auditing. Each chapter is supplemented with case studies, lessons learned, and challenges to consider. This book provides valuable insight that you can apply to your organization, whether you are well-versed in data analytics or just beginning.

About the Research

The IIARF and Grant Thornton surveyed CAEs, internal audit directors, data analytics managers, and other internal audit professionals across a wide range of primarily U.S. organizations from June 2015 to August 2015. Three hundred and sixty-six responses were received for the Data Analytics and Internal Audit Survey and another 28 for the Data Analytics and Leadership Survey. The survey results were supplemented with face-to-face interviews with more than 20 internal audit leaders and a number of focus groups. Insights from these professionals, who offered an in-depth look at their efforts to harness the power of data analytics, appear throughout the book in the form of best practices, lessons learned, and case studies.

As shown in **exhibit 1**, approximately 41 percent of survey respondents have at least six years of experience with data analytics, while more than 44 percent have fewer than three years' experience. Approximately 19 percent of respondents were introduced to data analytics within the past year. Regarding their internal audit careers, more than half say they have 10 or more years of experience in the profession. Respondents come from a variety of industries and organization sizes.

Exhibit 1: Survey Respondent Characteristics

Industries surveyed*

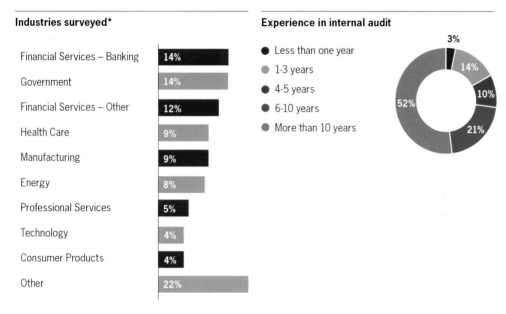

Financial Services – Banking	14%
Government	14%
Financial Services – Other	12%
Health Care	9%
Manufacturing	9%
Energy	8%
Professional Services	5%
Technology	4%
Consumer Products	4%
Other	22%

*Totals may not sum to 100% due to rounding.

Experience in internal audit

● Less than one year
● 1-3 years
● 4-5 years
● 6-10 years
● More than 10 years

3% · 14% · 10% · 21% · 52%

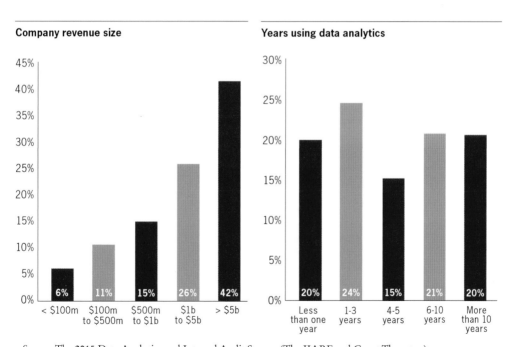

Company revenue size

< $100m	$100m to $500m	$500m to $1b	$1b to $5b	> $5b
6%	11%	15%	26%	42%

Years using data analytics

Less than one year	1-3 years	4-5 years	6-10 years	More than 10 years
20%	24%	15%	21%	20%

Source: The 2015 Data Analytics and Internal Audit Survey (The IIARF and Grant Thornton).

Chapter 1

WHAT DOES DATA ANALYTICS MEAN TO INTERNAL AUDIT?

Before using the Data Analytics Framework or attempting to have a meaningful dialogue about data analytics, internal auditors must understand what it means and how it applies to them. As with any technological concept, this term has evolved rapidly in recent years, resulting in a lack of precision that hampers professional use. With a clear picture of data analytics and its uses, internal auditors can be better prepared to integrate it into their internal audit function.

Data Analytics Defined

Put simply, data analytics is "the process of gathering and analyzing data and then using the results to make better decisions." Interviews with internal audit leaders reveal the following most popular attributes and components for the term data analytics:

- Analysis of operational, financial, and other data that quantifies and highlights risk and/or opportunity
- Data-mining information across multiple sources to provide actionable results
- Repeatable and automated processes that search for patterns and identify anomalies

The first two definitions tend to be common across internal audit departments. They include the analysis of organizational data to identify and mitigate risk or

> **KEY TAKEAWAYS**
>
> » The evolution of data can be defined by the four V's: volume, velocity, variety, and veracity.
>
> » Incorporating data analytics consists of five steps that can produce insights to support internal audit.
>
> » Depending on the desired outcome, four data analytics solutions—descriptive, diagnostic, predictive, and prescriptive—can be applied to synthesize data.
>
> » Case Study: Ace Hardware

improve organizational performance (e.g., the marketing department mines data to identify who is purchasing what product). The third, however, focuses on detecting exceptions through data analysis and has unique applications for internal audit.

> "Information is the oil of the twenty-first century, and analytics is the combustion engine."[1]
>
> —Peter Sondergaard, Senior Vice President, Gartner Research

The audit-specific definition for data analytics is consistent across the internal and external audit communities. The American Institute of Certified Public Accountants' (AICPA's) definition for data analytics in external audit—"the science and art of discovering and analyzing patterns, identifying anomalies, and extracting other useful information"[2]—is closely aligned with the attributes offered by the internal audit professionals we interviewed.

The Four V's of Data: Volume, Velocity, Variety, and Veracity

Data has existed for centuries in one form or another—from 500 years of climate data painted on cave walls to data that reside on today's distributed server platforms.[3] As data collection, recording, and storage have changed, so too have manual internal audit practices evolved into sophisticated techniques. These changes led, in part, to what is commonly referred to as data analytics, which has four unique attributes: volume, velocity, variety, and veracity.

Volume

Organizations now capture and process greater volumes of data than ever before. Only a few years ago, working with a 100-megabyte file was considered a lot of data. Today, data can be measured in zettabytes, or ZBs, which is equal to 1 trillion megabytes. Kathleen Sobieralski, professor and director of the Undergraduate Accounting Program at the University of Maryland University College, commented that although stakeholders hunger for more information within the organization, we are "drowning in data." The key sticking point is setting up the system around how to harness that data. Sobieralski notes that, although "The IIA has done a good job to bring data analytics and software tools to their audience, colleges are struggling to determine exactly how the software will be made available to them"—a tall hurdle to clear. For data analytics to provide value, organizations must develop data analytics infrastructures that can handle an appropriate volume of data.

> "We are drowning in information and starving for knowledge."[4]
>
> —Rutherford D. Rogers, American Librarian

Velocity

Beyond the vast amount of data collected, today's globalization and connectivity result in data produced at incredible and increasing speeds. IBM estimates that approximately 90 percent of all the data in the world was created in the past two years alone.[5] In 2012, 2.8 ZBs were created; in 2020, the total data generated annually is forecasted to reach 40 ZBs.[6] User-generated content such as photos and videos, and devices with sensors that constantly generate data—commonly referred to as the Internet of Things—contribute significantly to the mountain of digital information. Data velocity may have an inverse effect on internal audit's ability to analyze the critical data that requires a strategic focus on which data points are relevant and how to process the data, leading to value-add analyses.

> "Every day, three times per second, we produce the equivalent of the amount of data that the Library of Congress has in its entire print collection, right? But most of it is like cat videos on YouTube or 13-year-olds exchanging text messages about the next *Twilight* movie."[7]
>
> —Nate Silver, American Statistician

Variety

Data is being identified, captured, and stored from an increasing number of sources. From customer transactions to transmissions from outer space, the variety of data defies comprehension. Internal sources such as accounting, finance, and customer records have been complemented by the proliferation of external data sources. Today, data is categorized as structured and unstructured. Structured data is captured neatly in columns and rows, while unstructured data has no predefined manner or format[8] (see **sidebar, The Difference Between Structured and Unstructured Data**). According to global market intelligence firm International Data Corporation (IDC), unstructured data will account for nearly 80 percent of all enterprise data by 2017. To be successful going forward, data analytics must take into account differing types of data.

Veracity

This fourth "V" is the most frequently overlooked attribute of data analytics because it is often difficult to determine the quality or accuracy of data. For a data analytics implementation to be successful, the underlying data must be cleaned and normalized to limit the possibility of a "garbage in, garbage out" scenario. In other words, the data must faithfully reflect the truth. In organizations that lack a strong data governance culture, records can be incomplete, entries could have errors, and data might be inconsistently formatted. All of these issues can compromise analysis and produce inaccurate results.

The Difference Between Structured and Unstructured Data

Structured data exists in an understandable, organized format that allows it to be fed into a relational database management system for analysis. Operational data from an enterprise resource planning application, transactional data, customer data, financial data, and other data that include specific information (such as names, dates, addresses, and payment amounts) are all examples of structured data.

Unstructured data has no predefined organization format. It is typically in a free-form, text-heavy format that makes any type of in-depth analysis much more difficult. Examples of unstructured data include call center communications, open-text fields, contracts, audio and video, machine-generated data (server logs), blogs, and most social media feeds such as Facebook, LinkedIn, or Twitter). Email, for example, is indexed by date, time, sender, recipient, and subject, but the body of an email is an unstructured open-text field.

To derive useful insights from unstructured data, analysts must first prepare and transform the data—a time-consuming exercise in its own right—so that it may be structured and analyzed. According to *CIO Insight*, the steps to analyze unstructured data include first choosing only the most relevant sources, keeping in mind the goals and desired end result. It is critical that an organization's existing technology be able to support both the project's information architecture and the ability to process a real-time stream of data. Next, the data must be prepared for storage by removing noise such as blank spaces and symbols and then changing strings of text into formal language. Once the language is standardized, it is possible to establish relationships among sources and design a structured database where an analyst may use the frequency of named entities such as people, companies, and geographies "to understand the word pattern and flow into the text." Then the data may be classified, segmented, and fed into data analytics tools.[9]

The Evolution of Data Use

The broad objectives of internal audit—addressing governance and risk management concepts; confirming adherence to organizational policies, practices, and procedures; and evaluating internal control effectiveness—have not changed much over time. But the expansion of available information (data) and the development of software tools to analyze that data have had a substantial impact on how internal audit works toward those objectives while adding value to the broader enterprise.

Before the introduction of data analytics, internal auditors typically selected either random or judgmental samples. Data analytics allows for smarter sampling by identifying and highlighting anomalies or red flags, so analysts may choose to limit their data sample and review to those exceptions. Said another way, data analytics allows internal audit to migrate from sampling 25 transactions out of 1 million to 25 transactions out of 100. This combination of sampling and data analytics enables more meaningful analysis that is defensible from the outside looking in because decisions are evidence based.

Today, internal auditors can use data analytics to support their risk assessments wih tangible historical data. More substantive analytical procedures can address a wide range of risks by, among other things, helping internal auditors to better understand an entity and its environment and to perform more comprehensive tests for potential fraud. Analytics affords internal auditors greater precision in assessing the degrees of success in meeting defined objectives such as evaluating discrete pockets of information that cut through a larger process. For example, a data analytics test that identifies employees who are paid as vendors can provide initial evidence of fraud; that test can also lead to the implementation of controls and assist with remediation efforts.

The ability to supplement quantitative data analysis with qualitative research for added context marks a turning point in the evolution of risk management—and especially in internal auditing. In the past, internal auditors set an audit for a given operational area based on a prescribed cycle. Today, analytics can identify business areas that are high-control risks due to anomalous, nonconforming events and enable continuous monitoring of operations. A key development in this evolution is the ability to analyze unstructured data. Internal auditors can more easily and accurately leverage the unstructured data within a contract or invoice and supplement it with structured transactional data to perform unit cost analysis over time. If a contract includes a price list or specifies periodic price increases, an auditor can ensure that invoices comply with the contract by extracting and comparing those prices to the historical unit prices charged by the vendor. This example is not new to internal audit, but the application of data analytics results in a repeatable and automated process that is efficient.

Five Steps to Data Analytics

Data analytics allow internal audit to focus its resources on high-risk transactions and provide management with a higher level of operational assurance. This process has five fundamental steps, as shown in **exhibit 2**.

Exhibit 2: Five Steps to Data Analytics

Define the Question

Obtain the data

Clean and normalize the data

Analyze the data and understand the results

Communicate the results

1 Define the Question

An internal audit department must first define what it is trying to achieve and identify the anticipated value. One approach is to use an advanced analytics assessment, which begins with a business question, irrespective of the technology or complexity involved to answer a question. For example, an internal audit department might be asked to evaluate where potential fraud may be occurring and which parties may be involved. By beginning with the business question, multiple data sources can be selected for interrogation and analysis. The result of this exercise provides an initial path and helps to determine the technologies needed to execute the query.

2. Obtain the Data

The next step is to gain access to the data needed for analysis, a process commonly referred to as information discovery. Gaining access to data in a usable format can be difficult and expensive. The internal audit executives we surveyed identified obtaining data as the top challenge to incorporating data analytics into their internal audit functions (see **exhibit 3**). In mature companies, business units often use completely different IT systems, and exporting data through each application's reporting function is sometimes the only way to retrieve it. Complex IT systems, legacy IT systems, and business units that are overly protective of their own data can also present obstacles. However, today's data analytics tools include the functionality to identify the data to extract, normalize it, and validate it to a nonrelated source (e.g., validating the net amount from a transactional data set totals the sales total on a financial statement).

Exhibit 3: Top Challenges for Incorporating Data Analytics

Listed from most to least challenging

1. Difficulty in obtaining, accessing, and/or compiling the data
2. Time required to develop and execute analytic procedures
3. Insufficient resources or the need to train personnel
4. Lack of understanding about data analytics
5. Lack of management buy-in
6. Inability to interpret results
7. Other

Note: Challenges are ranked from most difficult to least difficult.
Source: The 2015 Data Analytics and Leadership Survey (The IIARF and Grant Thornton).
Question 8: Rank the top three challenges for incorporating data analytics into your internal audit function.

3. Clean and Normalize the Data

Cleaning data involves actions such as eliminating duplicative information and making sure that data fields with the same names from different systems are defined the same way. Forward-thinking companies have addressed the issue of data quality by instituting data governance programs with a committee charged with ensuring the integrity and usability of data throughout the organization. Like data governance programs, enterprise data warehouses—where data from disparate sources throughout an organization are integrated—can give internal audit a head start on clean data.

Normalizing the data (the process of organizing data to minimize redundancy and make it usable for a specific purpose) may be the most frequently overlooked step in the data analytics process. Anomalies—data points that are unexpected, peculiar, nonconforming, or otherwise not easily classified—might represent actual problems (or if your glass is half full, hidden opportunities). They might also be the result of peculiarities that are introduced as the data is gathered, recorded, or transferred from one platform to the next. In such cases, those peculiarities must be identified and corrected to enable analysts to make accurate conclusions. Most new software programs include modules that allow data analysts to spot and fix peculiarities more easily.

4. Analyze the Data and Understand Results

With clean data in hand, real analysis can begin. While the actual analyses differ depending upon the purpose of the inquiry, standard data analytics software packages can help complete the analyses. (See **appendix A** for a list of data analytics software tools prepared based on publicly available information.) Once the data is processed, the results must be interpreted. Anomalies must be studied to evaluate, for example, when an error has occurred or whether a feature in a system or process led to the result—and, if the latter, are the business process owners aware of the feature and its consequences? Internal audit will often trace results to the underlying source documentation (i.e., an invoice or purchase order) to confirm the nature, timing, and details of the event or transaction. At this stage, internal auditors review and refine the preliminary analyses based on the initial results and determine when nonconformance simply reflects an error or actually violates company policy. Even with careful analysis, data alone will not provide clarity on a specific control, requiring internal auditors to work closely with business units to interpret the results.

> "You can use all the quantitative data you can get, but you still have to distrust it and use your own intelligence and judgment."[10]
>
> —Alvin Toffler,
> American Writer
> and Futurist

The analysis stage is a fluid process that may need to be adjusted based on preliminary results. These results lead to additional and often customized analyses that will either provide support for an already understood theory or lead the analyst on a different path. A flexible analytics framework is critical.

5. Communicate the Results

Insights from data are worthless if executives are unable to grasp them. Of course, a failure to devote adequate resources to helping people truly understand the results of a data analysis (frequently manifested in dry tables full of numbers) can mean the failure of the entire program. Internal audit can slice and dice data and uncover compelling results, but without effectively communicating results, the analysis is not understood and often discounted. Data visualization (the graphical representation of data) is an innovative way to enhance decision-making because it permits the audience to understand the connection between disparate data sets and quickly see the big picture. Many off-the-shelf software data visualization packages have built-in tools that audit professionals can use to convey findings in accessible ways. Chapter 5 contains an example of an effective method of communicating and visualizing data analytics results.

CASE STUDY:
ACE HARDWARE—DATA ANALYTICS METHODOLOGY

Ace Hardware, a retailer-owned hardware cooperative with more than 4,800 locations and annual revenues of approximately $5 billion, employs a distinct methodology to determine how data analytics can be used to support internal audit tasks. By clearly defining what the analytics will accomplish and verifying that internal audit can access the data, Ace ensures that the foundational pieces are in place before devoting significant time. As part of this step, the team also defines what constitutes an exception; for instance, totals that significantly exceed budget from the prior year or transaction amounts that do not agree with source data. The data analytics step includes testing the accuracy of data, extracting the data, and then performing initial validation of results to identify data and/or logic flaws. With the analysis in hand, internal auditors work closely with the business unit leader to interpret the results, confirm initial findings, and delve into the root causes of exceptions. To get the most from an investment in data analytics, the team documents the process and develops a data analytics documentation standard that can provide a sufficient audit trail (e.g., Audit Command Language scripts) for future use of similar analyses (see **exhibit 4**).

Exhibit 4: Data Analytics Methodology

Define control objectives

- Determine relevant analytics
- Define exceptions
- Identify IT systems
- Verify access to data

Perform analytics

- Select appropriate data extraction tool
- Perform initial validation
- Confirm results

Report results

- Share results with business leader
- Identify root cause of exceptions
- Recommend process changes

Document process

- Update final workpaper
- Define resources to maintain repeatability
- Develop data analytics documentation standard

Note: This approach is intended to be a proxy example of a methodology and not a one-size-fits-all prescription.
Source: Ace Hardware. Used by permission.

Types of Data Analytics

Data analytics processes vary widely along a continuum of sophistication depending on how analysts intend to use the data, their knowledge of the technology and the industry, and their role within an organization. Some functions, including compliance or internal audit, are likely to focus on using data to determine what happened or why it happened, otherwise known as *descriptive* and *diagnostic*

> "If you torture data long enough—it will confess."[11]
>
> —Ronald Coase, British Economist and Author

analytics. These primary forms of data analytics might be useful to improve the efficiency of business processes and performance and inform strategic decisions. Other functions such as operations or sales are likely to take a more sophisticated approach. *Predictive* and *prescriptive* analytics uses data to determine what might happen and highlights actions that could influence those outcomes. The types of data analytics are not exclusive of each other, with the application of each driven by the intended task at hand.

Internal audit might use any or all of these types of analytics depending on its industry and goals. The following examination of the four types of analytics uses organizational examples to demonstrate the range of applications and reinforces the potential impact for internal auditors. Exhibit 4 provides guidance about when to use different types of data analytics, tailored to an internal audit department audience.

Descriptive Analytics

Descriptive analytics, the reporting of past events to characterize what has happened, is the least sophisticated and most frequently used analytics technique. It condenses large chunks of data into smaller, more meaningful bits of information, with little synthesis or analysis.[12] Descriptive analytics summarizes what happened and is the most basic underpinning of any Six Sigma program; for example, the manufactured goods industry has used descriptive analytics for decades to improve quality, boost output, and reduce waste. Descriptive analytics has formed the basis of complex modeling of manufacturing processes, associated systems, and even the supply chain that surrounds the manufacturing activity itself to simultaneously increase output and boost efficiency.[13]

A McKinsey & Company article highlights a precious-metal mine that used descriptive analytics to decode its complex processes and significantly increase yield.[14] The mine had a wealth of incomplete production and process data, and used descriptive analytics to reconcile inconsistencies and close data gaps. Once the data were complete and clean, the company was able to analyze a long list of process parameters and find which ones had the greatest effect on yield. By individually controlling one such parameter, the resulting increased yield added nearly $20 million annually to its bottom line.

Diagnostic Analytics

In addition to underlying transaction detail, diagnostic analytics can also provide insight into why certain trends or specific incidents occurred. Cutting data in different and deeper ways—for example, by product, region, or customer—enables analysts to gain a better understanding of business performance, market dynamics, and how different inputs affect the outcome. The consumer packaged goods industry and businesses that rely on Internet-based sales channels commonly use diagnostic analytics. The increasingly common practice of retargeting, for instance, is based on diagnostic analytics. Click on any product during an online shopping session and a diagnostic analytic will make certain that you see similar searched items wherever you browse next. Diagnostic techniques, however, are not necessarily specific to sales and marketing or any industry. For example, business operations can use diagnostic analytics to examine metrics by business unit and geography. This allows organizations to drill down into the granular details to identify which branch produces the most profitable product and the attributes surrounding that scenario.

Predictive Analytics

Predictive analytics allows users to extract information from large volumes of existing data, apply certain assumptions, and draw correlations to predict future outcomes and trends. For decades, retailers have been collecting data on individual buying trends and purchases and then using predictive analytics to improve sales strategies, pricing models, and distribution. One obstacle to pursuing predictive analytics is that it generally relies upon external data. For instance, while most retailers track customer purchases by product, few actually collect data on the attributes (e.g., temperature of the ZIP code to which a scarf was shipped) of the purchased products.

The benefits of predictive analytics can be significant. A global pharmaceutical company, for example, implemented a fraud-detection capability to pinpoint instances of improper use and distribution of pharmaceutical products. By analyzing conference and expense data housed in the remote servers, the predictive solution was able to identify government officials and employees whose profiles suggested a greater likelihood of fraudulent behavior. The ability to detect these trends and then highlight the specific transactions has helped the company improve its federal audit efforts.

Predictive analytics is not limited to commercial uses and is applicable for all organizations. For example, one public sector entity implemented a predictive modeling framework to detect and pinpoint the optimal usage of products and services to maximize health improvements for constituents. The solution maximized the return on investment for the client by quantifying the least cost combination of health products with the greatest improvement in patient health. The ability to detect and forecast the most effective services has greatly improved the client's ability to achieve its mission.

Prescriptive Analytics

Prescriptive analytics requires a significant volume of data to first make predictions and then link them to actions that will produce the best result. If predictive analytics seeks to determine "what the demand will be," prescriptive analytics answers the question, "How do I align my business to maximize profit if demand is 100 percent?" According to Grant Thornton's Anthony Hernandez, principal, advisory services, "Prescriptive analytics helps take subjective decisions into objective territory" using data to structure the decision-making process. The methodology features sophisticated algorithms to analyze potential decisions, define the potential connections between them, and forecast the likely impact of each decision. With this analysis, organizational leaders are able to build scenarios that help chart the best course of action.[15] Because prescriptive techniques are more complex, they are not commonly used by most functions.

One example of prescriptive analytics comes from the health-care industry. Health-care providers have traditionally been slow to adopt new technology; indeed, only 10 percent of health-care providers use advanced data analytics tools.[16] Many cite outdated or fragmented systems with limited connectivity that hinder the implementation of more sophisticated practices and keep the industry on the back end of the data analytics adoption curve. However, as more medical offices comply with the 2010 Affordable Care Act requirements for electronic health records, more health-care providers are moving to make better use of their data. Consider a health-care provider that forecasts demand for orthopedic procedures to increase by 30 percent over the next 10 years. Prescriptive analytics would be used to determine the optimal number of operating rooms, nurses, doctors (by type of procedure), and required beds to minimize costs and maximize use.

Internal audit departments are well positioned to capture value from advanced data analytics techniques. Their objective stance and wide purview allow internal auditors to see longer-term trends within the business. However, internal auditors and analysts must consider which analytic type is best suited depending on the business purposes (see **exhibit 5**).

Internal Audit Must Keep Pace with Advancements in Data Analytics

As organizations across all industries become more sophisticated, data analytics will be a critical tool to ensure that the internal audit function can help them improve their processes and controls. These more advanced data analytics techniques could help internal audit achieve more meaningful results. However, many internal audit groups are currently using these techniques indiscriminately without determining how data analytics can best meet their strategic needs. Instead, internal audit leaders must develop a vision as a first step for how data analytics can serve their organization and then ensure they have the people, process, and technology to execute effectively.

Exhibit 5: Four Types of Data Analytics

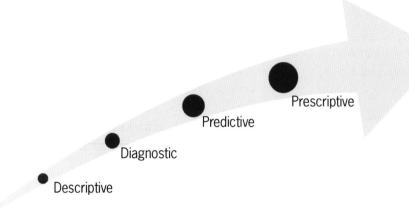

Analytic Type	Internal Audit Example
Descriptive	Analysis of accounts payable identifies all disbursements processed on Saturdays for over $1,000.
Diagnostic	Analysis of accounts payable identifies John Smith from Dallas as the accounts payable manager who approved each Saturday disbursement over $1,000.
Predictive	Analysis of accounts payable in multiple cities identifies all Saturday disbursements over $1,000 and assigns common attributes to each occurrence (e.g., number of total vendors, employee tenure, and total accruals booked each month).
Prescriptive	Analysis that builds and tests scenarios around different policies to determine what course of action would lead to a drop in the number of disbursements over $1,000 processed on Saturdays.

Chapter 2

THE DATA ANALYTICS FRAMEWORK

Now that we have painted a picture of how internal audit professionals can be better prepared to integrate data analytics into their function, let's take a closer look at a framework the researchers developed to provide concrete steps to enhance data analytics capabilities in an internal audit environment (see **exhibit 6**).

Exhibit 6: The Data Analytics Framework

Develop a Vision

Evaluate Current Capabilities

Enhance People, Process, and Technology

Implement, Monitor, Evolve

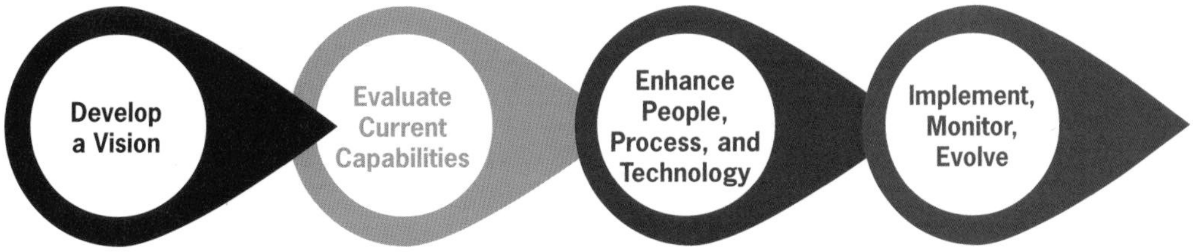

Source: The IIARF and Grant Thornton.

Step 1: Develop a Vision

The first step in the Data Analytics Framework is to develop a vision for how data analytics will support internal audit. According to the research, internal audit professionals use data analytics for four primary tasks:

1. Compliance

2. Fraud detection and investigation

3. Operational performance

4. Internal controls assessment

To develop a data analytics vision that drives adoption by the entire organization, internal audit must consider broader organizational goals, balance short-term investments with long-term vision, and identify ways to gain the assistance of operational management and process owners. This requires a detailed understanding of the following yet-to-be-recognized benefits of data analytics: to increase efficiency, increase effectiveness by performing whole-population testing instead of random or judgmental sampling, provide greater audit coverage, and realize significant cost savings, to name just a few. **Exhibit 7** identifies what internal audit professionals recognize as the benefits of data analytics.

Exhibit 7: Benefits of Data Analytics

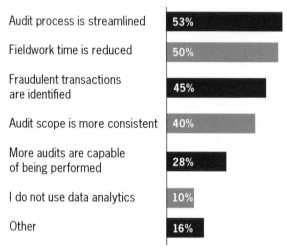

Source: The 2015 Data Analytics and Leadership Survey (The IIARF and Grant Thornton). Question 2: What benefits do you derive from using data analytics? Select all that apply.

Once the benefits of data analytics are identified, a vision of the future can be crafted and an execution strategy developed. Ideally, a data analytics vision can be used to develop a detailed (yet flexible) three- to five-year road map to transform the vision into reality.

Step 2: Evaluate Current Capabilities

A successful data analytics effort consists of three interlocking and dependent components—people, process, and technology. Each internal audit group should assess its current capabilities in these three areas. To assist with assessing the process, the researchers created a Maturity Model Framework that resulted from survey results and the interviews and focus groups that were conducted. This self-assessment diagnostic tool allows the internal audit group to categorize its current people, process, and technology into one of five evolutionary steps:

1. Ad hoc

2. Defined

3. Repeatable

4. Institutionalized

5. Optimized

Enhancing people, process, and technology strategically and cohesively allows internal audit to develop into the sought-after "optimized" maturity level.

The Maturity Model Framework can also serve as a basis for comparisons with peers, a resource "needs" plan, and a development plan for personnel skillsets. Used properly, this framework measures movement up the maturity curve to data analytics value by defining expected outcomes. This helps internal audit leaders build the business case for investments in data analytics by convincing enterprise decision-makers to provide support (i.e., additional resources) to reach increased functionality. Chapter 4 takes an in-depth look at the Maturity Model Framework.

Step 3: Enhance People, Process, and Technology

To improve internal audit's performance, strategic investments should be made to: 1) enhance the skills and experience of personnel; 2) get the right data in the right form to perform analytics; and 3) discover the software combination best suited for the vision—the three drivers for a successful implementation of data analytics. Internal audit skills can be advanced through training, targeted hiring, or by augmenting talent using external resources. To gain access to data, internal audit must engage leaders across the organization for support, including collaborating with IT personnel. Additional resources and executive support are critical, as the Data Analytics and Internal Audit Survey found that just 43 percent of respondents felt they had the necessary budget to support the use of data analytics. In addition, potential access obstacles must be identified and plans designed to navigate them successfully. Once the skills and experience reach requisite levels and access to data has been achieved, an assessment of data analytics tools and technology should be performed to identify which technology path best enables the vision.

Step 4: Implement, Monitor, and Evolve

Get started, periodically measure your progress, and be prepared to evolve your data analytics program to match the stated vision. Data analytics will continuously change in the future with advancing technologies and larger sets of disparate data. A data analytics implementation program is essentially a change management initiative, so management buy-in and support are critical factors to ensure long-term success. By gauging progress on key metrics and sharing results and impact with the executive team and board of directors, internal audit can maintain the momentum necessary to achieve its vision.

Over the next few chapters, we will take a deeper dive into each of the four steps of the Data Analytics Framework, discussing each in detail.

Chapter 3

DEVELOP A VISION: UNDERSTANDING HOW DATA ANALYTICS WILL SUPPORT INTERNAL AUDIT

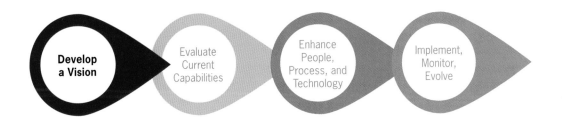

Before preparing to embark on a journey to deploy data analytics to improve company performance, it is important to formulate a data analytics vision. Internal audit leaders should be aware of how comparable departments currently use data analytics and try to identify their successes and challenges. With this information, they can develop a detailed road map to manage the vast opportunities associated with data analytics programs, along with the related costs, the current and growing obligations of internal audit, and any challenges (such as personnel constraints) to realizing the vision.

Many of the CAEs interviewed have taken some level of action toward incorporating data analytics into their organizations. While some efforts are still being developed, others are more mature and continue to gain traction. Regardless of an organization's data analytics maturity level, most internal audit departments expect their new capabilities will lead to more thorough audits and actionable recommendations. Simply having a detailed plan is not enough. To translate it into

KEY TAKEAWAYS

» Internal audit departments currently use data analytics for four primary tasks: compliance, fraud detection and investigation, operational performance, and internal controls.

» To develop a data analytics vision, CAEs must consider three strategic factors and understand the projected benefits.

» As a next step, CAEs should develop a detailed three- to five-year road map to translate the vision into action.

» Case Studies: Martin Marietta, Discover, KeyBank, and AmerisourceBergen

action, CAEs must get buy-in from the C-Suite and management by clearly articulating how data analytics can deliver tangible benefits throughout the enterprise. This chapter introduces the benefits of data analytics—greater efficiency, stronger conclusions, more effective risk mitigation, and measurable financial results—that will be used to develop the blueprint around the data analytics vision.

How Internal Audit Uses Data Analytics

Internal audit departments are increasingly using data analytics in response to increased demands, available technology to increase efficiency and effectiveness, and an ever-increasing presence of new risks. Despite this

> "Data really powers everything we do."[1]
>
> —Jeff Weiner,
> CEO, LinkedIn

progress, most departments have merely scratched the surface of what is possible. Internal audit departments have deployed data analytics to respond to high-priority areas, which can differ markedly by industry, regulatory pressures, and department capabilities. The uses for data

analytics in internal audit fall into four common categories: compliance, fraud detection and investigation, operational performance, and internal controls (see **exhibit 8**).

Exhibit 8: Common Uses of Data Analytics by Internal Audit

Internal Audit Function	Data Analytics Use Examples
Compliance	Evaluate expense reports and purchase card usage for all transactions. Perform vendor audits by utilizing line-item billing data to identify anomalies and trends to investigate. Assess regulatory requirements (e.g., receiving an alert when the words "pay to play" are noted on an expense report—could be indicative of a Foreign Corrupt Practices Act violation). Identify poor data quality and integrity around various data systems that are key drivers to (non)compliance risks.
Fraud Detection and Investigation	Identify ghost employees, potential false vendors, and related parties or employee-vendor relationships. Highlight data anomalies that pose the greatest financial and/or reputational risk to the organization. Investigate symptoms of an asset misappropriation scheme to answer the "who, what, where, when" questions.
Operational Performance	Isolate key metrics around spend analysis (e.g., payment timing, forgone early-payment discounts, and payment efficiency). Perform duplicate payment analysis and recovery. Perform revenue assurance/cost leakage analysis. Perform slow-moving inventory analysis. Identify key performance and key risk indicators across industries and business lines.
Internal Controls	Perform segregation of duties analysis. Perform user access analysis. Assess control performance. Identify potential outliers that would indicate control failures or weaknesses.

Internal audit departments devote most of their time to operations and compliance. In an IIA Pulse of Internal Audit Report released March 2015, North American CAEs indicated that auditing operational risk (23 percent) and compliance/regulatory risk (14 percent) were their top priorities. Another form of regulatory compliance, the U.S. Sarbanes-Oxley Act of 2002, made up 12 percent of audit plans. By contrast, business strategy accounted for just 6 percent of the overall plan.[2]

At companies in heavily regulated industries such as finance and health care, internal auditors are struggling to keep afloat amid a steadily rising tide of new regulations. A 2014 Grant Thornton survey of CAEs found that 36 percent of respondents indicated the focus on regulatory compliance has prevented them from devoting resources to higher-value activities.[3] If a large portion of internal audit's budget is already committed to regulatory compliance, the CAE has much less flexibility or resources to invest in other areas.

CASE STUDY:
THE EVOLUTION OF MARTIN MARIETTA'S DATA ANALYTICS PROGRAM

Martin Marietta Materials, a publicly traded building materials company with a market cap of $10 billion, has an internal audit department that has been using data analytics since 2007. According to Cesar Perez, vice president of internal audit, the audit department identifies specific tests that will provide the greatest benefit and then determines how often to perform each test (for example, annually, quarterly, or monthly) based on the level of risk. Those analytics may change over time, depending on the realized results.

Some of the greatest benefits have come from analytics around accounts payable and purchasing. The tests included comparing tax ID numbers in the vendor file to the Social Security numbers in the employee file for matches, analyzing vendor master file information for anomalies, and searching for duplicate payments. Martin Marietta management determined that it could achieve the appropriate coverage for these risks by implementing additional controls. An example of this was the creation of system reports to monitor for duplicate payments before they are made. By performing analytics in a variety of areas and then narrowing them down using a risk-cost-value approach, Martin Marietta is able to allocate time and resources for data analytics to higher-priority activities. In addition, analytics help reduce the amount of time it takes to perform recurring audits by identifying specific transactions to test.

Discover Financial Services, a global Fortune 250 company with annual revenues of more than $7 billion, clearly understands the need to apply data analytics (as opposed to random or judgmental sampling) to real-time transactions. According to Jeff Song, director of internal audit, his team is constantly seeking to identify the transactions that cause the greatest risk and are candidates for further investigation. Discover starts with broad parameters and, after identifying which attributes are driving false positives, fine-tunes its analytics model until a small subset of exceptions are identified. The exceptions are investigated in a collaborative process with IT and the business unit.

Discover has built a team with members whose perspective extends beyond data analytics. In Song's experience, the ideal data analytics auditors understand the business they are auditing, are detail-oriented and analytical, and have a strong working knowledge of data management and data interrogation techniques.

A key to Discover's success with analytics is that internal audit lets business units know at the outset that the data analytics scripts used as part of the audit will be turned over to them after the audit is completed. This transparent, proactive approach has resulted in a collaborative environment in which the business unit is invested in analytics because they understand the value it can deliver.

Developing a Vision for Data Analytics

The most effective visions seek to answer well-defined questions such as, "What are the top issues facing the organization?" and "How can internal audit add more value?" The answers to these questions help develop the data analytics vision, which should be achievable, aspirational, and filled with "small wins" that lead to a long-term objective. For example, a CAE might set a target of increased automation of repeatable processes, using data analytics for specific types of audits, and working on higher-value work or streamlining processes. To do so, the CAE must construct a vision that includes three overarching concepts: 1) align with organizational goals; 2) balance short-term obligations with long-term gains; and 3) communicate progress.

Align with Organizational Goals

CAEs must have a solid understanding of their organization's overall business strategy to ensure their data analytics vision supports it. A 2015 report developed by The IIARF finds that more than half (57 percent) of practitioners say their internal audit department is "fully or almost fully aligned with the strategic plan of their business."[4] This task may be easier to accomplish in organizations where the CAE participates in strategic planning and key management initiatives.

In companies with little collaboration and ongoing dialogue between internal audit and the C-Suite, the internal audit department must work closely with management to gain knowledge of strategic vision and key initiatives. Opportunities include participating in the annual risk assessment process by conducting interviews with executives and key stakeholders. These one-on-one discussions provide an open forum to discuss overall organizational strategy as well as the direction for individual business lines. This periodic dialogue can help to drive collaboration between management and internal audit, and the resulting insight will form the foundation of the data analytics vision.

Balance Short-Term Obligations with Long-Term Gains

An internal audit department should evaluate where best to focus their investments. Many factors shape an internal audit department's priorities, such as the industry and the organization's maturity. Ultimately, every data analytics effort, large or small, requires an investment in time, money, and personnel, forcing internal audit to weigh short-term costs against long-term gains. Chevron's Mario Boffa, group manager of corporate audit, describes how Chevron "viewed data analytics as the logical next step in the continuous evolvement of its risk assessment and audit planning process." Boffa says this initiative took significant time and manpower to build and implement, but internal audit management viewed the exercise as an investment for the future. "We are already seeing positive results," he added. "Audit teams are reporting that the new standardized data analytics reports have reduced field work time and expense, resulted in more targeted audit scopes, and identified recoveries we would potentially not have identified using standard sampling techniques."

If an internal audit department is already overwhelmed by its current tasks and responsibilities, its leaders might struggle to take a more strategic view of the department's long-term needs. It is critical to move beyond a reactive, transactional approach. Internal audit departments should define a future state, the successes it will realize, and how data analytics directly supports that future state.

Communicate Progress

While the early stages of a data analytics effort—when internal audit must purchase new tools and hire new staff, or train existing staff, to use them—may introduce some short-term inefficiency, the long-term benefits of data analytics are clear. Increased use of data analytics might be one of the best ways for internal audit to cover more ground without adding staff. However, our research indicates that a lack of resources remains the most common impediment to the increased use of data analytics in internal auditing.

Emphasizing collaboration and using existing resources in an enterprise is one way to ease the financial burden. For example, a data analytics program may include the need to automatically extract and store data in a database or business warehouse. Other departments, such as finance, may also find a business warehouse and reporting tool useful, providing an opportunity to partner and share budget money for a more collaborative effort. Momentum will be gained when executive management and departments outside of internal audit start to understand the benefit of data analytics.

CASE STUDY:
KeyBank—Defining the Data Analytics Vision

In many organizations, a self-assessment of past practices combined with a highly regulated external environment leads to change. The financial services industry may be the best recent example of this combination. In response to a quality assurance review performed in 2012, KeyBank (a regional retail and commercial bank with more than 13,500 employees) determined that implementing data analytics into its audit function would reduce enterprise risk, provide greater coverage, and drive efficiencies throughout its service lines. To accomplish this goal, KeyBank hired Elvis Kanlic to create and lead its newly formed data analytics team and oversee its strategic implementation.

According to Kanlic, KeyBank outlined the following factors of a successful integration of a data analytics strategy:

a. A sound data analytics plan structured as a strategic multiyear program: iterative in nature and broad enough to modify or enhance prior deployments.

b. A business case with long-term goals and a corresponding road map to achieve those goals.

c. Supporting milestones that are realistic and provide clear expectations and accountabilities of phase deliveries to all stakeholders, including senior leadership.

d. Metrics to track progress and understand areas of strength as well as areas that need improvement.

These components can be distilled into a tangible mission statement, says Kanlic: "The data analytics function will develop and execute automated solutions that drive broader coverage and increase efficiency in the audit process." The mission would be supported by more specific and tangible elements:

a. Develop a risk-based plan that focuses on reviews driven by account and transactional data.

b. Integrate data analytics to automate test procedures by collaborating with engaged teams.

c. Assess data integrity and quality validation procedures conducted by lines of business for all critical reporting.

d. Transition automated solutions to operate in a continuous monitoring environment where the performance of key controls provides insights for risk intelligence on a predefined frequency.

e. Conduct periodic reviews of the organization's data management and governance functions.

Kanlic credits the strong support from the broader technology organization and his cross-functional staff as the two key factors in propelling the data analytics initiative forward. Along this journey, KeyBank has learned several critical lessons in making the initiative successful:

a. Highlight the value proposition of data analytics to the business units.

b. Identify a staffing model that incorporates continuing education based on desired skills.

c. Communicate the program's progress through a value-based and metric-focused approach.

KeyBank's data analytics program has established a solid foundation to build upon and continues to develop and enhance automated solutions that falls within one of the three primary delivery streams:

a. Ad hoc analytics: Point in time, attribute-driven population extracts, statistical samples, and exception reports for various engagement teams.

b. Integrated analytics: Data analytics team is integrated in all major phases of the review. Analytics are customized to automate review objectives and are designed to perform on a repeatable basis, requiring only minor modifications for any subsequent analysis.

c. Continuous analytics: Integrated analytic solutions are selected and moved to perform continuously, based off of a schedule (e.g., monthly, quarterly, etc.) or event (e.g., credit card payment reversed). Continuous analytics results are used to assess the performance of key controls (continuous auditing) and support risk intelligence processes (continuous risk intelligence).

The Benefits of Data Analytics

A successful strategic vision must clearly define the benefits that internal audit—and the entire organization—will capture through this multiyear journey. Quantifying the data analytics value to business leaders can be challenging, in part because the term *data analytics* is frequently misunderstood. It should not be viewed as a stand-alone solution but rather a change in the organizational approach that will produce results. To deliver value, data analytics must be performed by team members with technical and business knowledge and supported by processes that enable access to quality data. As stated in *The Wall Street Journal*, "If the analysts don't know the business and the questions to ask, the company risks running down a lot of expensive dead ends . . . it's always crucial to insist on the basics of sound analytical practice. And to remember: numbers can tell you things you never even knew to ask. But they never speak for themselves."[5]

According to the 2015 Data Analytics and Leadership Survey, internal audit functions that have integrated data analytics into their operations point to a number of tangible benefits: a majority of respondents cited streamlined processes, nearly half noted a reduction in time spent in the field, and more than one-quarter pointed to increased audit capacity. These benefits fall into four broad categories.

Greater Efficiency

Although the core objectives of internal audit have not changed, the use of more powerful software allows internal auditors to decrease the level of human involvement in the data aggregation, review, and analysis—and be substantially more precise in assessing operational performance. More broadly, the patterns, trends, and relationships that data analytics pinpoints can help firms to quickly identify new business opportunities, optimize spending, and deploy personnel more strategically. Software programs are able to perform multiple model permutations on data so that exact patterns can be quickly discerned. For example, data analytics can determine whether invoices over $500 are handled differently than those for lesser amounts, enabling internal auditors to identify the issue, analyze the root cause, and determine appropriate next steps.

Internal auditors who apply data analytics can quickly filter out false positives and adjust analyses so the results are more meaningful. For example, credit card companies have such safeguards in place to quickly identify potentially fraudulent transactions, automatically pinging customers with a notification to check in on their account.[6] This greater efficiency enables internal auditors to focus their energies on higher-value-added activities as defined by their department, organization, or regulator.

Better-Informed Decisions

Typically, internal audit will work closely with external auditors in the hopes of preparing the organization for a smooth external audit. As the AICPA points out, data analytics can contribute to every phase of an audit, beginning with an enhanced understanding of an organization and the environment in which it operates. This step can help internal auditors determine which departments or processes would receive the most benefit from this approach.[7]

By eliminating random or judgmental sampling and offering better proof to support assertions, data analytics helps businesses generate stronger conclusions and leads to better informed decision-making. Mark Pearson, director of internal audit at Packaging Corporation of America, stated, "If we are able to say that we tested the entire population of payments in a year for specific attributes and found no issues, it's far more powerful than saying we selected a statistical sample. In many cases, testing the whole population provides more assurance than the old style of small samples." Many of the main benefits derived from the use of data analytics stem from the ability to move away from sampling and toward testing entire data sets.

Risk Mitigation and Monitoring

Data analytics provides the potential for an internal audit department to increase its value to its organization by identifying, managing, and monitoring risks more effectively and efficiently. Software programs geared toward internal audit purposes have prepackaged modules that detect errors, fraud, and inefficiencies. Possible disruptive events can be recognized and prevention strategies enacted. All of these steps allow businesses to engage in stronger risk-based, comprehensive, and objective decision-making. When talking about compliance risk, Elizabeth Truelove McDermott, vice president of audit, ethics, and compliance services for DeVry Inc., stated, "We view data analytics as critical to our mission. Our regulatory projects are now 100 percent population driven—including our annual Title IV Department of Education audit—and we leverage data analytics to assist us in performing that work." The ability to use data analytics to monitor risks and identify where to apply resources will transcend internal audit and grow into a core competency of the entire organization.

For example, the internal audit department of a leading service provider to the utility industry worked closely with IT and operations management to automate and implement data analytics scripts used during an audit to detect outlying transactions for fuel procurement cards. Every week, the eight-factor fuel exception report is automatically generated and emailed to frontline managers so they can review their respective crew's fuel purchases and identify unusual spending patterns. This process of active monitoring and inquiry of purchase anomalies has significantly reduced the number of exception transactions for the organization. Many data analytics applications offer multiple predeveloped routines to run against standard data sets, as well as the ability to develop custom routines based on specific applications or business processes and tailored for an individual organization's data stores. These routines can detect exact duplicates or fuzzy duplicates, outliers, and gaps; they can also perform word-list searches and mathematics-driven Benford analysis.[8] The data analytics tools or the related scripts can be configured for periodic audit-based analysis or even for continuous monitoring of a data set, enabling internal audit and the business to move to a proactive, preventive monitoring strategy, further reducing the risk of disruptive events.

Measurable Cost Savings

Data analytics offers internal audit the tools to measure and demonstrate its own financial results. Andrew Schmidt, vice president and director of internal audit at health-care industry solutions provider AmerisourceBergen, notes: "Our main goal is to mitigate risks, but the natural outcome of that is dollar savings—it's just a byproduct of what we do. When we talk about our budget with our CEO, it's easy because we have data to show our results every year. High-volume transactions and margins drive these savings. Before SAP it was difficult, even painful, to do this, but now we have the right tools."

In many cases, internal audit can turn over successful data analytics routines to business units to manage continuous-monitoring processes. Routines to identify duplicate payments and inventory anomalies can result in significant cost savings at little additional expense to the enterprise. By operationalizing and essentially sharing its data analytics capabilities, internal audit can not only reinforce its value to the organization but also enable business units to improve their performance.

Bringing the Data Analytics Vision to Life: Developing the Road Map

With a solid vision and understanding of the benefits of data analytics, internal audit can outline a road map for how the department can move forward. The road map, which should cover a three- to five-year period, lays out the steps and timeline to translate the vision into reality. It breaks down the implementation into phases that build upon an internal audit function's existing assets sequentially and strategically. Each phase should include clearly defined goals and metrics to determine when those goals have been met, as well as the capabilities and investments that will be needed.

When developing a road map, internal audit must ensure that it delivers tangible value to the organization. Launching a data analytics program involves an initial outlay of time and resources, and a well-developed road map can help internal audit secure funding. Every road map should acknowledge current conditions (the starting point), outline the future state (the destination), and include realistic supporting milestones. These components serve to highlight the distance that must be covered as well as the benefits that will accrue.

Inherent in the road map is the need to pinpoint investments and tradeoffs necessary to achieve certain outcomes. To identify the potential benefit of data analytics, internal audit should recognize that it is not merely a risk mitigating exercise but also will reduce costs and add value beyond the department.

The data analytics vision for internal audit can paint a very compelling picture for how the function can better serve the organization and potential value it can contribute. It should be aspirational, longer term, and flexible enough to adapt to changing needs as the organization evolves. And the vision should energize and inspire internal audit professionals to conceptualize how their roles will expand in the coming years. Once a CAE develops a road map to translate this compelling vision into reality, the next step is to determine the internal audit department's existing assets—the people, process, and technology.

CASE STUDY:
KEYBANK IDENTIFIES BENEFITS OF IMPLEMENTING DATA ANALYTICS INTO INTERNAL AUDIT

Risk Mitigation

- Improved risk assessments
- Better deployment of resources to highest-risk areas
- Test 100 percent of transactions for many controls
- Use of data analysis for sample selection in cases where testing 100 percent of transactions is not possible
- Deploy fraud detection and prevention procedures

Cost Reduction

- Efficient coverage of the organization's risk areas
- Minimized disruption to the business during the execution of internal audit reviews
- After initial investment in the program, potential to reduce audit hours in subsequent years

Value Add

- Ability to reallocate budget to more value-added activities
- Leverage data analytics for internal and external benchmarking
- Quantification and root cause analysis of issues noted
- Ability to generate more relevant background information for audit reports

This exercise can enable internal audit leaders to evaluate potential strategies and gain a better understanding of the required resources and expected outcomes. Because data acquisition costs can significantly alter the return on investment for certain initiatives, internal audit should conduct periodic assessments of the organization's data management and governance functions.

CASE STUDY:
AMERISOURCEBERGEN'S LONG-TERM VISION FOR DATA ANALYTICS

AmerisourceBergen Corporation is a global distributor of pharmaceutical products and provider of related goods and services with more than $130 billion in annual revenues. It has more than 16,000 employees, just 20 of whom work in internal audit. Andrew Schmidt, vice president and director of internal audit, credits data analytics for giving the team the ability to analyze millions of transactions on a continuous basis: "Data analytics is a core tenet in each audit we perform; we are not pulling random or judgmental samples but rather choose our samples based on what the analytics tell us." As with any internal audit department, AmerisourceBergen's primary focus is risk mitigation and providing assurance to management and the board of directors. However, the team's approach seeks to include the metrics that stakeholders find critical.

Schmidt explained that AmerisourceBergen makes a point to quantify every finding and observation. That way, internal audit is not just identifying control weaknesses but also mapping it to the true financial impact. In fact, this approach has identified and collected $35 million in profit-and-loss opportunities over the past five years, more than offsetting the cost of the audit department. With the ability to provide tangible results to the C-Suite and the board of directors, internal audit is able to obtain the budget it needs for training and acquiring advanced technology to make the department even more efficient.

Internal audit has become more than just a watchdog, it is also a consulting partner with the business units. For example, when the department identifies an exception in product pricing or a rebate program, the business unit is notified so the appropriate adjustments can be made. This consultative mindset allows internal audit to bridge the gap from auditor to adviser. In fact, the business unit has asked internal audit to provide consultative services (usually involving data analytics skills), and the department has issued a non-audit-driven management letter of its analysis. Schmidt estimated that approximately 20 to 30 percent of the audit team's workflow is dedicated to management consulting projects, which in turn make the audits run more efficiently and allow for greater coverage across the organization. A good portion of their data analytics work also goes toward assisting their external audit team, which helps keep the audit fees down. Significantly, internal audit maintains independence with various controls and processes when performing management consulting projects.

As an enterprise, AmerisourceBergen is developing its predictive business intelligence capabilities primarily targeted at revenue and customer generation. Schmidt hopes that his group's data analytics team can become more centralized to share best practices and tools and be deployed on various projects throughout the organization. He believes that this insight will allow internal audit to tap into advanced techniques that incorporate nonfinancial and macro-level data and broaden the types of analytics and results that can be achieved.

AmerisourceBergen's next step is to integrate data visualization using industry-recognized tools and provide a continuous monitoring environment to business units that internal audit can use on the back end. The goal of this effort is to detect real-time trends and resolve issues on a continual basis. This capability would enhance the cost savings and allow internal audit to focus promptly on predefined areas throughout the year, as opposed to a set schedule.

AmerisourceBergen attributes its success in using data analytics to the following factors:

- C-Suite and audit committee communication and support. (Once you can show them the power of identifying anomalies and P&L savings, they endorse the concept.)

- Start by hiring someone to be the dedicated data analytics person. ("Everyone thinks they want to be the data analytics guru, but you have to build a cross-functional team with specialties for each component," Schmidt says.) The ideal person should have a financial, audit, and IT background. ("They need to love being in the detail and good with data and systems.")

- The tool and process to obtain data is important. Access to ERP native system source data (at the transaction level) without involving IT is critical. AmerisourceBergen has a robust process (which IT approved) through a SAP/ACL software stack.

- Create a quick win to drive momentum and gain buy-in from the appropriate people. ("This will allow you to acquire the right people, the right technology, and the flexibility to get creative.")

Chapter 4

EVALUATE CURRENT CAPABILITIES: PERFORMING A DATA ANALYTICS SELF-DIAGNOSTIC

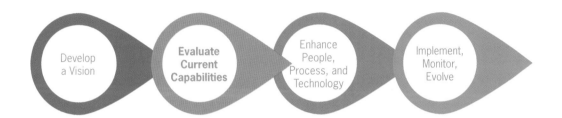

Develop a Vision | Evaluate Current Capabilities | Enhance People, Process, and Technology | Implement, Monitor, Evolve

Once a vision for how data analytics can serve internal audit is articulated, the next step is to determine the department's progress in building data analytics capabilities—and what steps must be taken to elevate performance.

The good news is that many internal audit functions have taken at least some initial steps on the data analytics journey. The survey found that nearly 90 percent of internal audit departments are using data analytics in some capacity, suggesting that these respondents have established a foundation upon which to build. But internal audit professionals know they should be doing more; 69 percent of respondents said that they wish their organization would place a greater emphasis on data analytics. See **exhibit 9**.

For their part, CAEs have a clear desire to unlock the potential of data analytics for internal audit. Mark Pearson of Packaging Corporation of America said, "Data analytics ought to be a key part of our risk assessment and planning to make

KEY TAKEAWAYS

» A successful data analytics effort consists of three interlocking components—people, process, and technology—as well as access to the necessary data.

» Internal audit must assess its department's capabilities in these three categories to discover where to improve.

» The Maturity Model Framework, a proprietary diagnostic tool based on this book's research, outlines five progressive stages for internal audit departments.

» Case Studies: Sherwin-Williams and University of Texas System

it more effective." Mary Ann Tourney, CAE at CF Industries, said, "We are moving toward using data analytics for substantive testing, but our organization still has some work to do."

Exhibit 9: Need for More Focus on Data Analytics

Do you wish your organization would put more focus on data analytics?

● Yes

● No

● My organization places the right focus on data analytics

28%

3%

69%

Source: The 2015 Data Analytics and Internal Audit Survey (The IIARF and Grant Thornton).

The challenge in adopting data analytics is that it requires a multifaceted approach. Technology is an enabler, but as with any technology-based solution, talent and process are needed to execute the strategy. The research revealed that an organization's maturity is determined by its vision for data analytics in three categories: people (the ability of internal audit team members to embrace data analytics); process (the method an organization uses to access data and integrate it into its daily tasks); and technology (the platforms, systems, and tools that enable data analytics).

The research revealed that process maturity varies widely from one internal audit function to another. A department's performance is dependent on its capacity to gain access to the data needed to support analytics. But securing the universe of data is not enough; internal auditors must also know where to focus and why. Those decisions drive how to apply specific analytics tools. Internal auditors who start with the questions that need to be answered can condense the data set, helping them avoid boiling the ocean to find what they need.

The sophistication of tools in use, however, varies considerably (see **exhibit 10**). Visualization, deployed by more than one-third of respondents, straddles several analytics categories (descriptive, diagnostic, predictive, and prescriptive) but is currently used primarily as a presentation tool—and is thus underutilized. On the other hand, modeling and predictive analytics are less frequently used, likely because they require both more powerful software and a deeper understanding of the data and its applications.

Exhibit 10: Top Internal Audit Uses of Data Analytics

Analyzing trends	72%
Compliance monitoring	56%
Detecting fraud	54%
Evaluating business/ operation performance	48%
Data visualization	40%
Predictive analytics	17%
Modeling	12%
I do not use data analytics	10%
Other	7%

Source: The 2015 Data Analytics and Internal Audit Survey (The IIARF and Grant Thornton). Question 1: Identify how you currently use data analytics. Select all that apply.

Overall, these results reinforce that internal audit typically has some foundational assets upon which to build. However, internal auditors must ensure their department has the right mix of people, process, and technology to get the greatest benefit from data analytics.

Maturity Model Framework

The analysis led to the development of the Data Analytics Maturity Model Framework, which defines five phases of data analytics maturity based on internal audit's assets and capabilities in the categories of people, process, and technology (see **exhibit 11**). This framework can be used as a scorecard to help internal audit departments determine where they fall along this continuum. By determining their performance in each category, internal auditors can pinpoint where they need to enhance their capabilities.

A department can move up the maturity curve by defining expected value, technology capabilities, adoption process, and required budget. In this respect, the framework can help internal audit leaders build the business case for investments in data analytics by directly connecting additional resources to increased functionality.

Exhibit 11: The Data Analytics Maturity Model Framework

Category	Ad Hoc	Defined	Repeatable	Institutionalized	Optimized
People	Dedicated internal audit function with limited data analytics skillset	Capability to "borrow" data analytics expertise from other departments Use cases understood and prioritized by staff Data governance framework established and understood by staff	Dedicated data analytics staff in internal audit with advanced capabilities (e.g., CAATs) Established success metrics around desired skills Continual training requirements specific to data analytics	Dedicated data scientist within internal audit Developed strategy for additional capabilities Road map for implementation across enterprise Direct link from activity to risk mitigation understood and applied Performance metrics include data analytics	Dedicated data scientist within internal audit and significant number of other internal auditors with data analytics skills Risk coverage, profiles, and other constraints captured and used to optimize scheduling Compensation connected to data analytics skillset
Process	Small sample sizes Inconsistent reporting Heavy reliance on IT to obtain data Process does not leverage prior audits and lessons learned	Large sample sizes Consistent reporting Established data access protocol with IT Process leverages historical lessons learned on a limited basis	Significant sample sizes Standard reporting Data verification and accuracy protocol established Process applies a standardized approach that incorporates historical lessons learned	Significant or all data audited Continuous auditing throughout internal audit function Reporting shared across stakeholders Root-cause understanding of exceptions Process is continually enhanced based on lessons learned	Real-time data monitoring with alerts Continuous monitoring throughout business function Real-time reporting accessed through self-service business intelligence Closed-loop process to measure success and value Process to change root causes to alter outcomes
Technology	Spreadsheets	Other reporting and relational databases Data visualization tools (limited basis)	Data access on demand Data interrogation scripts are defined Workflow and data capture technology Data visualization tools used for reporting	Access to central enterprise data store Automated scripting and testing Data visualization tools integrated for data input, analytics, and reporting	Automated data extraction, transfer, and load (ETL) Advanced analytics available for use within function System information management (SIM) software

Source: The IIARF and Grant Thornton.

While each phase in the Maturity Model Framework includes specific criteria and capabilities for the use of data analytics, it represents the ideal. In reality, when internal auditors use the framework to gauge their department, performance within the three categories could fall across the five phases of data analytics maturity. For example, internal audit could have access to advanced data analytics tools (thanks to its organization's adoption of technology), placing it in the "repeatable" phase, but have audit professionals who have little knowledge of or interest in data analytics, making them "ad hoc." By giving a clear idea of how an internal audit function performs in each category, the Maturity Model Framework can help CAEs make targeted investments in people, process, and technology where it will have the greatest impact.

When using the framework, it is important to view these three asset categories holistically rather than in isolation because, in practice, they are intertwined, reflecting how dramatically the business landscape has changed in recent years. Technological advancements have increased the prevalence of automation, data generation, and robotics, as well as the availability of and access to data.[1] Each of these elements has had an impact on the people and process needed to carry out routine and advanced tasks. While capabilities can be measured for each category, understanding how strengths in one category create opportunities in the others is crucial; for example, streamlined processes to harness new technologies can reorient the team's focus. Similarly, internal auditors attuned to data analytics can get more from existing tools.

Without team members who are conversant in data analytics, internal audit may not know which data sources to secure. Without the right process, the data that the department obtains may be incomplete or compromised. And without the right technology, internal audit may lack the tools to retrieve data or glean insights. Internal audit's ability to analyze both structured and unstructured data increases as it becomes more advanced across these three categories, particularly in technology.

Maturity Model Framework Phases

We interviewed internal auditors who lead departments across the spectrum of the Maturity Model Framework. The following paragraphs highlight the characteristics of each stage along the framework.

Ad Hoc

At the lowest end of the maturity curve are internal audit departments that have yet to reach the starting line. These functions perform their activities with technologies that have been available since computing power became commonplace. Resources with data analytics skills are not available, sample sizes are typically small, and data manipulation occurs in entry-level applications such as Microsoft Excel.

Internal audit functions that use data analytics on an ad hoc basis have certain common characteristics: the department is overrun with day-to-day tasks and has adopted a reactive stance, which limits its ability to change or thrive. Still, its current practices address controls, risk mitigation, and fraud at an acceptable level, so audit professionals lack an understanding of how data analytics tools can add value.

Data Analytics

Defined

Internal audit departments in this category have established a data governance framework to attempt to aggregate inconsistent data distributed over various sources within the organization. Overall, internal audit professionals have a clear understanding of the areas where data analytics can have an impact, and the department has developed a protocol to secure the data it needs to use larger sample sizes and perform consistent reporting. This groundwork enables the function to incorporate best practices from external parties and secure resources from data analysts around the organization.

The research revealed that some practitioners at this level have integrated visualization software to translate analysis into accessible forms, with the belief that finding patterns in larger data sets increases productivity and efficiency while making the analysis easier to communicate. Organizations aggregate data in relational databases to generate those reports.

Repeatable

Going from defined to repeatable is a significant step, because internal audit must integrate data analytics to support some of its day-to-day tasks and processes. A department at this level has established success metrics (such as productivity increases, required sample sizes, testing, and reporting results) that directly quantify the benefits analytics can provide. Data governance and integrity measures are tracked and improved upon.

Practitioners typically gain access to data on demand through a shared database and/or data automation. Departments use workflow and data capture technologies to accommodate large sample sizes in the testing and have established protocols for data verification. Dedicated data analytics resources are available and apply advanced analytics tools to identify trends and anomalies. Additionally, the internal audit department applies data analytics concepts to gain internal efficiencies with tasks such as risk-based sampling, data reconciliations and integrity reviews, and rule set validations.

Institutionalized

Currently, relatively few internal audit functions have made it this far along the maturity curve. These organizations have institutionalized analytics into their audit practices and established regular touch points to update strategy, check progress against their road map, and provide metrics that directly link activities to their value in mitigating risk and detecting fraud.

Departments in this category routinely include the entire data set in testing for a majority of audits, use continuous audits in strategic places to push alerts to the proper process owner, and identify and understand the root causes of exceptions. Investments in technology have made data readily available, with automated scripting and testing in place through audit software. In addition, tools to support reporting, visualization, and trending are in widespread use.

Optimized

At this time, this category is primarily aspirational and represents the next step for the highest performers. Internal audit departments that ascend to this category will use advanced analytics to a high degree of effectiveness. A dedicated data scientist within internal audit works with audit staff that are highly versed in data analytics to develop queries to support specific tasks, and data from across the enterprise is readily available thanks to extract, transfer, load (ETL) software. Together, these capabilities enable the department to incorporate a continuous auditing environment to detect exceptions and anomalies in real time. An optimized internal audit department has incorporated unstructured data into risk assessments seamlessly and is spanning new internal audit risks like cybersecurity through the application of system information management (SIM) software. The internal audit department works with business unit leaders to help them implement the tools and process needed to support continuous monitoring on a business-unit level.

Internal audit has built processes to measure performance and engage in regular sessions to determine how performance aligns with the data analytics vision. This emphasis on strategy and planning enables it to use software and tools to support continuous improvement efforts, creating a virtuous circle of accuracy, efficiency, and higher performance.

CASE STUDY:
SHERWIN-WILLIAMS—BUILDING MOMENTUM FOR DATA ANALYTICS

When Sherwin-Williams began its data analytics journey, the greatest challenge was accessing, normalizing, and understanding the data it has—and the data it needs. As the organization obtained data and performed analytics, momentum was gained around the initiative by communicating "small wins" to executive management that would be far reaching. Specifically, internal audit identified opportunities to increase profits through earlier identification of root causes of inventory variances and other cost savings opportunities at the individual manufacturing facilities. Sherwin-Williams hopes to apply those findings (and solutions) on an enterprise-wide basis to maximize its profit potential.

Following is a sampling of internal audit's milestones thus far:

4. Full population analytics resulting in evidence-driven observations and value-add recommendations

5. Enhanced analytics-based risk assessment driving a more efficient audit process

6. More than 25 analytics built to detect suspicious transactions and operational inefficiencies

7. Approval for two full-time employees to focus exclusively on data analytics

Sherwin-Williams plans to build on this success by using data analytics to address cyber risks and mitigate international exposure around the Foreign Corrupt Practices Act (FCPA) of 1977 and third-party vendors.

Greater Maturity Delivers Added Benefits

Although most internal audit departments are in the early stages of adopting data analytics, the most mature functions have started to reap the benefits of advanced analytics. Research suggests that two data analytics elements will be crucial to the future of internal auditing: continuous auditing (owned by internal audit) and continuous monitoring (owned by the business unit). Both are designed to help internal audit operate more effectively by testing transactions in near-real time, reducing risk for the entire organization.

Internal audit will likely help business units set up their continuous monitoring environment by identifying key risk and performance indicators. It will be consultative in setting up a program or a process to receive the benefits of continuous monitoring while remaining objective and independent from the business unit. Once a structure of continuity is in place, the incremental coverage and risk mitigation efforts that internal audit reaches should skyrocket.

Continuous Auditing in Action

Continuous auditing is defined as the automated performance of an audit activity on a regularly repeated basis that gives timely insight into an organization's risk and control issues. This method migrates stand-alone automated analytical solutions to perform on a predefined frequency based off of a schedule (monthly, quarterly) or event (for example, a dollar threshold or an action such as expense reversal). A designated engagement team contacts and monitors results and reports discrepancies to business unit managers. In this way, internal audit can review business areas and determine if controls are effective in managing risk.

To determine where continuous auditing would have the greatest impact, internal auditors can use the following four factors as a checklist:

- Inherent and residual risk level: Is the area rated high risk to moderate high risk?

- Critical focus area: Does the organization or regulatory bodies consider this area critical to growth and sustainability?

- Cycle frequency: Is it on the upcoming schedule, and which teams are engaged in the review?

- Unsatisfactory reviews: Did the last review result in significant issues and unfavorable results?

Functions or specific tasks that meet these criteria can be streamlined significantly by implementing continuous auditing capabilities.

Continuous Monitoring in Action

Continuous monitoring is the automated review of business processes and controls and is typically owned by business management. In a 2013 report, The IIA defined three lines of defense in risk management: 1) operational management, including internal controls; 2) risk management and compliance functions; and 3) internal audit.[2] Continuous monitoring is part of the second line of defense and provides a regular, automated review of the effectiveness of established business controls and the quality of the transactions within them. By monitoring business process systems and focusing on controls and transactions, automated continuous monitoring helps an organization detect errors, fraud, abuse, and system inefficiencies timely. The key element of transitioning a control monitoring system to the business unit will be the business unit's realization and acceptance.

Continuous Monitoring in Action

Internal audit departments that implement continuous monitoring can cover more ground by automating routine processes and intervening when anomalies or exceptions are detected. The following examples highlight the types of activities and transactions that continuous monitoring can perform:

Identifying Potential FCPA Violations

- Payments made to a high-risk organization.
- Payments received from a foreign bank account.
- Payments to a professional services firm where no prior relationship existed.
- Payments with a description such as "facilitation," "gifts," "for services rendered," "cash," "government expense," or that are blank.
- A vendor is doing business with a company or individual that is on the World Bank Blacklist.
- A vendor is operating in a country that is ranked "high risk" by the Corruption Perceptions Index.

Employee Expense Fraud

- Year-to-year expense submission comparison by employee.
- Expenses incurred on dates when the employee was not working (such as week-ends, holidays, and vacation).
- Expense totals are just under a specific review threshold.
- Excessive reimbursement amount by similar employees within the same department.
- Duplicate expense amounts submitted within a certain time frame.
- Round dollar amounts on expense submissions.
- Benford's Law analysis on expense submissions.
- Excessive expense submission by expense category.

In general, internal audit is in the very early stages of harnessing data analytics. Most functions have focused on using it for descriptive and diagnostic purposes, and are in the process of gaining better access to data sources throughout the organization. Similarly, internal auditors are becoming more acquainted with the applications for data analytics, but many have yet to become conversant and relatively few have expertise in both audit and analytics.

Despite the increased emphasis on data analytics and its potential value, organizations have been struggling with several obstacles—limited access to data, disparate systems, consistent and usable data, access to appropriate tools and technologies, a lack of resources, and a shortage of talent—to incorporate analytics more fully into operations. The research revealed that internal audit's views on analytics tend to mirror the organization as a whole; if the organization lacks a central strategy to adopt analytics, the internal audit department follows suit. Bucking this trend will require strong leadership from the CAE and coordinated efforts involving other departments. Without an organization-wide "champion" who has both the incentive and authority to effect change, data analytics plans will likely fail to gain the necessary support.

> "Data is the kind of ubiquitous resource that we can shape to provide new innovations and new insights, and it's all around us and can be mined very easily."[3]
>
> —David McCandless, British Data Journalist

Using the Maturity Model Framework, internal audit leaders can pinpoint the investments they can make to increase their department's level of sophistication. By adding selected tools or refining certain processes related to data aggregation and analysis, CAEs can significantly increase internal audit's capabilities. In an era of finite resources, the challenge is to assess the costs and tradeoffs to achieve the maximum impact.

CASE STUDY:
UNIVERSITY OF TEXAS SYSTEM

The University of Texas (UT) embodies many of the best practices that internal audit should emulate to capture the benefits of data analytics. They are in the early stages of evolving data analytics throughout the internal audit organization.

The UT System is one of the nation's largest systems of higher education, with eight academic and six health-care institutions that educate more than 217,000 students annually. With 20,000 faculty and more than 70,000 health-care professionals, researchers, student advisers, and support staff, the UT System is also one of the largest employers in the state. As a higher education system, UT must address some of the same challenges that the largest global corporations also face: managing the heavy burden of regulatory compliance (due to strict rules in areas such as research grants and financial aid); aggregating data from disparate technology platforms across the UT System; and ensuring that employees throughout the internal audit organization understand the role that data analytics can play in delivering improved audit efficiency and audit coverage.

UT CAE Mike Peppers has the daunting task of overseeing and auditing the system's multiple institutions. To aid in this effort, in 2014, Peppers spearheaded the development of a three-year strategic plan to integrate data analytics more fully across the audit organization enterprise-wide. Centralized data analytics support is provided to internal auditors across the 14 institutions and provides for some common audit reporting for data that may be decentralized at the individual institutions. This effort involved an initial assessment on data access and quality and a meeting between internal audit professionals and the data owners at the institutions to identify data sources, ensure quality, and reinforce the importance of data access to the organization's overarching goals.

Because most individual institutions cannot support a full-time person dedicated to data analysis on their own, Peppers assigned a subject matter expert (SME) to direct the data analytics program, develop the strategic plan, and provide ongoing advice and guidance to all institutions. The SME is assisted by a data analytics specialist with an internal audit background who works with pilot initiatives (such as procurement card analysis) and individual institutions to map data sources. UT's structure is not common: typically, employees throughout an organization do not have access to a dedicated data analytics specialist.

Data quality is an issue: each institution has its own systems, so before data can be used, it often must be converted to different formats (for example, data normalization). With a common tool set across the organization, UT recognized that it would also be able to standardize training and information sharing across the entire organization. UT has adopted software (IDEA) to create common data connectors and make the data more accessible and usable.

While UT does not include the use of analytics in its core performance metrics, it expects the internal auditors to adopt these tools. Internal audit also sent out an Analytics Master Program that it could incorporate into any audit. For example, recently UT used its analytics tool to classify expenditures for a report that the University of Texas at El Paso submitted to the National Collegiate Athletic Association (NCAA). Other institutions followed suit and were able to streamline the audit process. Peppers emphasized that they need to continue to communicate more success stories relating to data analytics to illustrate why these tools should get adopted and motivate the institutional auditors to do something new and different that improves audit results and coverage. Although UT is ahead of the curve in its efforts on data analytics, Peppers does not believe the organization is doing anything earth-shattering—nor does he believe they are finished. Recently they shared with their audit committee examples of graphical representations from a comprehensive set of data analytics that was extremely well-received by the executives who would like to see more of the same. He notes, "Two to three years from now, we are going to be doing a lot more than we are today."

ENHANCE PEOPLE, PROCESS, AND TECHNOLOGY: THE KEY INGREDIENTS TO DATA ANALYTICS IMPLEMENTATION

Subsequent to both developing a well-articulated vision for the incorporation of data analytics in the internal audit function and performing a self-evaluation of where the internal audit department falls along the Maturity Model Framework, CAEs should identify specific needs and evaluate any gaps in resources. Implementing a data analytics framework typically requires capital investment in two critical areas: talent (acquisition and development) and technology (software and hardware). Meanwhile, departments must devote time and resources to improving processes to secure data.

The enhancement of people, process, and technology is critical to data analytics adoption, yet each component carries unique challenges. For example, internal auditors often resort to using more familiar technology tools. Chevron's Mario Boffa said, "The future of tools includes ACL, but people use whatever they are comfortable with. We used to push ACL a lot, but over time people would go back to Excel or Access." This tendency points

KEY TAKEAWAYS

» To improve performance, internal audit must make strategic investments in talent, process, and tools.

» The internal audit team can be augmented through training, targeted hiring, or by using external resources.

» To gain access to data, internal audit must devise processes to address common obstacles.

» Internal audit must be saware of the increasingly powerful range of data analytics tools that are currently available.

» Case Study: American Heart Association

to the importance of preparing and upgrading department staff to ensure follow-through on the data analytics framework.

Even departments that have successfully implemented data analytics recognize the need for continued improvement and training. "We hope to accomplish a more robust training program," said Mike Peppers, CAE of the University of Texas System. "There's no reason that people can't use the tools or software. The garden-variety auditor needs to get comfortable using those tools."

Internal audit departments that have the right team and software can still lack access to data. The challenges vary by organization, but internal auditors commonly struggle with poor data quality, inaccessible data, or data whose complexity requires enterprise-wide systems or governance to harness properly.

In the Data Analytics and Internal Audit Survey, only 44 percent of respondents think their organization dedicates a sufficient budget to the use of data analytics (see **exhibit 12**). Even though obtaining additional budgetary resources may be difficult, internal audit groups should clearly articulate how data analytics can reduce costs in the long term through the improved effectiveness of internal audit and enhanced operational efficiency. Baylor Scott & White Health Vice President of Internal Audit Monica Frazer explained, "You can't sell a lot of resources to management on this unless you have examples of value; you have to first get enough to do pilot work to demonstrate that it is useful and more would be valuable."

Exhibit 12: Budget Sufficiency for Data Analytics

How much do you agree with the following statement? "My organization dedicates a sufficient budget towards the use of data analysis."*

- Somewhat or strongly agree
- Neither agree or disagree
- Somewhat or strongly disagree
- My organization does not use data analytics

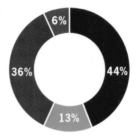

Source: The 2015 Data Analytics and Internal Audit Survey (The IIARF and Grant Thornton).

While internal audit departments have historically struggled to obtain additional budgetary resources for data analytics, there are positive indications in the market that more organizations are recognizing the benefits of data analytics. In a 2014 Grant Thornton survey,[1] 41 percent of internal auditors said their budget would increase in 2014, while just 15 percent said their budget would decrease. In addition, 26 percent of respondents projected staffing increases, while just 8 percent projected decreases.

Although every internal audit function has unique needs, the following discussion will provide audit professionals with a deeper understanding of the people, process, and technology required to meet the expectations of their organization's senior leaders.

Building an Effective Team

Regardless of the level of adoption of data analytics in the internal audit function, the function must ensure its team has the proper training and capacity to implement the data analytics strategy. To promote success in the strategy, internal audit should identify professionals with a mixture of audit experience and familiarity with data analytics. According to the research performed for this book, organizations are either a) teaching auditors data analytics skills; b) teaching accounting concepts to data analysts; or c) using a team approach where different individuals have the requisite skillsets. A recent global survey of internal audit professionals found that while approximately 60 percent had an accounting background, just 10 percent had education in technology or computer science.[2] Organizations can achieve this diversity in skillsets by either developing their existing team or augmenting staff through new hires or external vendors. The proper path depends on the internal audit department's needs, goals, and the current state of staff knowledge.

Developing Your Staff

Many organizations embrace training programs focused on data analytics skills for internal auditors. As noted earlier, the Data Analytics and Internal Audit Survey revealed that an overwhelming majority of respondents (88 percent) are interested in enhancing their data analysis skills. However, not all CAEs see the development of all internal auditors on data analytics as a viable goal. Internal auditors who have little exposure to data analytics can lack the critical thinking needed to glean insight from the results. Monica Frazer explained, "What has not worked is when we tried to train every auditor on analytics. You need a certain mindset to do this." AmerisourceBergen's Andrew Schmidt shared a similar sentiment: "You need a team. When we tried to train our whole staff in data mining, we were unsuccessful. So instead, we have three experts who do the heavy lifting and get the right data to the audit staff."

While training every internal auditor to have a deep knowledge of data analytics might not be practical or advisable, at the very least each should be conversant in the possibilities. "Everyone in internal audit should be aware of what the different tools can do so they can recognize a situation in which it would be beneficial and then bring in another person to actually use the tool," Frazer said. Finally, to drive development, data analytics should be aligned with the organizational goals through the performance reviews and compensation structures of the organization. This measure sends a clear message that the organization places priority on data analytics and it will continue to become an increasingly critical element of the internal audit department's capabilities.

Acquisition of New Staff

When screening candidates, organizations should place a premium on identifying individuals who are creative and critical thinkers with the desire to move comfortably in both the internal audit and data analytics worlds. Since data analytics is both an art and a science, creative thinkers can find innovative ways to connect the dots.

The IIA's Global Technology Audit Guide 16[3] provides basic definitions of job descriptions for personnel in the internal audit and data analytics realm. CAEs should, at a minimum, evaluate whether their team structure contains the skillset detailed in the following descriptions:

- Data specialist: A member of either internal audit or IT with a detailed understanding of IT infrastructure, data sources, and how to access that data.

- Data analysis specialist: A member of internal audit trained in a given technology tool.

- Staff internal auditors: All team members must have a general understanding of data and data analytics software.

- Leadership: To streamline oversight, the CAE and other department leaders must be fully aware of the functions that have been automated or are dependent on data analytics software.

Determining a Structure for Data Analytics Resources

From an organizational standpoint, CAEs must evaluate where to place data analysts within the enterprise to obtain the greatest return. The following three models were considered by KeyBank during its implementation of data analytics, with each having its own benefits and related costs:

Centralized: When analysts are part of a freestanding team, they can benefit from knowledge sharing through apprenticeships within the centralized team. In addition, they can provide support during peak periods. The challenge is that management and audit may be misaligned, which can result in erratic project schedules.

Decentralized: Analysts who are embedded in each division can gain first-hand, specialized business knowledge and also reduce management overhead. The hazard is that once assigned to business units, they may have less time to devote to audit requests.

Hybrid: By maintaining a centralized data analyst team and SMEs in each department, internal audit can cover critical functions and ensure that development extends beyond the core team to the SMEs. The hybrid model often requires additional effort for training and quality assurance—not just in internal audit, but also on the part of each division.

To determine the best model, CAEs should evaluate their team members, the department's needs, and the use of data analytics across the organization.

CASE STUDY:
HOW THE AMERICAN HEART ASSOCIATION PLANS FOR CO-SOURCING TO AUGMENT INTERNAL STAFF

The American Heart Association (AHA) recognizes the need for data analytics in its internal audit approach and methodology. As a not-for-profit organization, AHA must protect its integrity and reputation with limited resources. It uses analytics to detect suspicious transactions, identify anomalous travel and entertainment expenses, and reduce its sampling population by honing in on the high-risk areas. Vickie Tesmer, AHA's director of audit and consulting services, stated that the biggest barriers to progressing down the data analytics path are rapidly changing technology, the risk of losing indispensable staff, and the cost of maintaining tools and training.

AHA plans to co-source with a third-party vendor specifically trained in data analytics to supplement its in-house data analytics methodology. This approach will allow them to "turn on and off" their advanced data analytics needs via co-sourcing and continually stay current with emerging trends, industry best practices, and new technologies. With a co-sourced approach, AHA feels confident that it will be able to expand its current capabilities to address not only the traditional audit risks but also the increasing concerns around social media, privacy, and cybersecurity.

Tesmer indicated that the ability to obtain support for a co-sourced relationship stems from her direct line of communication to the audit committee and executive management (with regular updates on their data analytics initiative), maintaining a working relationship with IT, and building a tangible business case for why data analytics is both a risk and cost mitigation activity.

Ensuring Open Communication Between Internal Audit Staff and Dedicated Data Analysts

Currently, many smaller departments lack a dedicated data analyst, instead relying on a resource within other departments such as IT. By contrast, larger internal audit functions may already have a separate data analytics group. In such instances, the analysts are well-versed in systems, coding, and writing queries but typically have little firsthand knowledge of internal auditing. When audit professionals make specific requests of data specialists, it can result in ambiguous results and even missed opportunities. For example, one internal auditor examined results from a data analytics query and identified 20,000 exceptions. Upon further analysis, the apparent anomalies were actually caused by a feature in the payroll system; when the query was written, the programmers were not aware of it. This example highlights the need for internal auditors to work closely with analysts to devise and interpret queries.

A potential solution includes a structured onboarding process in which the internal auditor and data analysts ensure the end goal is understood and the approach is agreed upon. Incorporating a communication flowchart with approval recommendations allows internal auditors to have more visibility to the data and realign efforts midstream, as opposed to when an extract or analysis is considered complete. The step will take an investment in time and training on the front end, but long-term results will be more accurate, thereby driving efficiency.

Securing the Data You Need

As the Data Analytics and Leadership Survey revealed, one of the greatest obstacles internal audit departments face when using data analytics is a lack of access to the *right* data sources. A critical component of any data analytics framework is building a smooth process to obtain data. Following are three challenges to acquiring usable data:

1. Complex Data Sets and the Need for Customized Extraction Tools

To get data from existing sources, analysts must develop a script set. If internal audit does not have a technical resource to execute the request, it can cause delays and increase the transactional cost of locating data. In addition, databases may also require specific extraction tools. Many organizations have at least one ancient system and just one person in the enterprise who really knows how to access the data, creating a bottleneck for requests.

2. Poor Data Quality

Beyond quantifying the level of effort required to get the data, internal audit departments must also evaluate whether the data will be of sufficient quality. For example, if only 70 percent of the information is populated in any given field or the data is not standardized, then the effort to format and scrub the data may outweigh its usefulness. When encountering these issues, internal audit departments should seek to identify the process deficiencies that are causing the data quality issues and implement the necessary process improvements.

Feeder systems—the systems from across the organization that populate the enterprise resource planning system—can provide data at a summary level, thus missing many of the data elements internal auditors require. In these cases, internal audit must pull from two separate systems to get the desired data. Access to summary and related detail from one or more enterprise resource planning systems is necessary to understand the full picture. In accounts receivable, for example, summary data would be revenue by customer while the related details are the revenue lines on an order and customer address. Enterprise analytics provide the ability to seamlessly relate summary content to the underlying detail and analyze data within and across business functions.

In addition to gaps in level of detail, data may come in an incompatible format that cannot be read or imported by standard tools. Although tools exist to address these issues, organizations must have a resource who understands how to use the given tool.

3. Data Accessibility

In some systems, the only way to obtain data is to run the software's own canned reports and then export them. Data cannot be accessed from the system's back end because it is either locked by the software company or is in the cloud with no way to gain full access. In this situation, internal audit has two options: run multiple reports, export the results, and then join the data together; or have the software company build custom reports to suit the organization's needs. Neither choice is universally optimal. The internal audit department should consult with the IT department, inspect the license agreement with the software provider, and address the topic through vendor management.

Unlocking the potential of data analytics depends on knowing what data is available, how to access it, and how much it costs to access it in a usable format. This task calls for a more active role for the internal audit department as an evangelist for data analytics. In persuading leaders of business units or functions to share their data, the CAE should emphasize the benefits to them—in the form of greater transparency into operations and the opportunity to identify ways to elevate performance.

Asking for the Data You Need

Most internal auditors are not properly trained in extracting data, but asking the proper questions at the outset can avoid common issues in the interpretation and analysis of the results. The following elements should be included in any request:

- Format
- Sample fields
- Data dictionary
- System file layout
- Intended use of data
- Control totals to verify completeness
- Owner of the data input process
- Limitations to the data

Choosing the Technology You Need

A significant upfront cost for certain internal audit departments is the purchase and implementation of the technology platform that supports the data analytics effort. Several types of data analysis tools are available and applicable to the work of internal auditors—though the optimal tool will depend on the required functionality and availability of data.

The technology currently used by internal audit departments varies widely in complexity and functionality (see **exhibit 13**). In the Data Analytics and Internal Audit Survey, 77 percent of respondents reported using Microsoft Excel for data analysis, while 53 percent deploy computer-assisted audit techniques (CAATs) such as Audit Command Language (ACL) and IDEA, and 37 percent use Microsoft Access. More than 10 percent of respondents indicated that other tools, including SQL, Tableau, and SAS, are part of their arsenal. However, only a handful of respondents have adopted tools such as TeamMate Analytics, Monarch, ActiveData, Oversight, SPSS, EnCase, Arbutus, ActiveAudit, EZ-R Stats, and Forensic Toolkit ("FTK").

Exhibit 13: Data Analytics Tools Used by Internal Audit

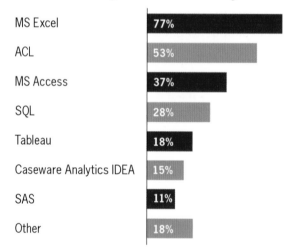

Source: The 2015 Data Analytics and Internal Audit Survey (The IIARF and Grant Thornton). Question 8: What data analysis tool(s) does your organization currently use? Select all that apply.

This section examines the major categories of available data analysis tools, detailing the types of data the software can handle and scenarios in which it delivers the most value. The categories are presented in order of usage by internal audit, with the most common discussed first. Armed with this baseline of knowledge, internal auditors can further explore the tools that fit their needs.

Selecting the Appropriate Tool to Meet Your Objective

Determining the best tool for a given analysis or audit test is not as simple as asking, "How much?" or "What type of data will be analyzed?" The specific objective should be the primary factor in selecting the appropriate software tool. Organizations should avoid bringing in the equivalent of a bazooka when a fly swatter will suffice. Based on experience and conversations with CAEs during this product's development, several important considerations emerged:

- Can the tool be linked to a production system so that the data can be obtained on demand?
- Is the tool cross-functional (i.e., able to cleanse, validate, test, and visualize data)?
- What is the total cost of ownership (including purchase price, maintenance, licensing, and employee training, among other factors)?
- How quickly can employees get up to speed?
- Can the tool access structured and unstructured data?
- Can the tool be hosted on the cloud? Considering vendors and tools with both on-premise and cloud solutions provides more options.
- What tools are already being used by other departments? Before purchasing a new tool, CAEs should communicate with other executives and managers to evaluate whether other departments use tools that could be expanded to internal audit.

Typically, a combination of tools, rather than just one solution, can help departments gain the capabilities to integrate data analytics into their operations. For example, a product specializing in data visualization may have to be combined with software that handles data preparation and integration to optimize the benefits to the organization.

Spreadsheets

Internal auditors use spreadsheets. As the most basic level of software, spreadsheets offer several features that are employed by internal audit departments, including calculation tools, graphing tools, pivot tables, ability to connect to external data sources, and built-in functions for querying data. Many third-party providers have started making "add-ins" for entry-level products that extend the software's data analysis functionality. Essentially, the add-ins supercharge the existing application with statistical and engineering tools and other features to support analysis.

Spreadsheets are often used to perform data analyses, calculations, modeling, or graphing on structured data. Such applications include financial modeling and analysis, for which spreadsheets are particularly useful because they can reference other cells and pages in a given workbook; for example, an auditor may create a running balance tally in a spreadsheet. Spreadsheets are not suited for more complex analyses involving multiple types of data, currency neutralization, or large data sets. However, they are ideal for reporting—taking data that has been analyzed in a more sophisticated program and displaying results in an easy-to-open file.

While spreadsheets are appealing for their return on investment, simplicity, and familiarity—indeed, spreadsheets are universal across internal audit—they also contain inherent risks such as potential for accidental errors (data integrity), limited access restrictions, and limited change management controls. Many organizations have experienced material weaknesses in internal control over financial reporting because of an overreliance on spreadsheets that were not appropriately controlled. In one case, a company spent three years untangling a mess caused by users introducing errors into master financial spreadsheets and baking those errors into future reports.

Within the industry, the general consensus is that spreadsheets are an approachable entry point and a valuable tool as part of a suite of software. But using them in isolation is an outdated approach insufficient for handling the volumes of data that internal auditors work with today.

Computer-Assisted Audit Techniques

CAATs have a wide range of uses within internal audit, investigations, management accounting, and general inquiries. Specifically, these software tools analyze data to highlight potentially fraudulent transactions, compliance issues, and internal control weaknesses. Survey respondents cited CAATs as the second-most used type of technology tool. Interviews with CAEs found that most internal audit departments use CAATs every day.

CAATs can help the user analyze a large swath of electronic financial and nonfinancial information. They enable the extraction, sampling, and manipulation of data to identify symptoms of errors, problems, specific issues, and trends. In addition, one of the key benefits of CAATs is that the original information cannot be altered once imported, a feature that helps to preserve data integrity and limits user errors. These tools maintain logs of all analyses and queries performed on the data to maintain an audit trail of the user's procedures. The logs can then be used to automate future analyses through the use of macros (i.e., a repeatable and automated process that is recalled upon user command).

Other common features include built-in functionality to help the user perform specific analyses quickly and easily. Key query functions include data stratification, sample extractions, missing sequence identification, statistical analysis, calculations, duplicate transaction identification, pivot table creation, cross-tabulation, and data visualization. These programs offer the flexibility of creating virtual fields for analysis and calculations and custom queries, which are especially useful in addressing specific risks.

Database Management System

A database management system (DBMS) captures and stores data. A general-purpose DBMS enables users to create and define databases, perform queries, and update data sources. They are ideal for storing extremely large structured volumes of data, such as banking transactions and health-care data that are too large to fit on a local computer drive. However, certain types of DBMS software have record, or size, limitations. Besides the potential for large storage capacity, a DBMS can also be designed for convenience and performance to enable data visualization.

Two features highlight the utility of a DBMS. First, internal auditors can input a large volume of data, perform queries, and be presented with a manageable number of records to analyze. Second, a DBMS allows internal auditors to join data sources that are not necessarily intended to be combined. For example, logs of physical key card access history records can be cross-referenced with the organization's payments register, both of the data sources being maintained in a DBMS. An internal auditor on the hunt for symptoms of fraud can then cross-reference the physical key card access history data to evaluate if irregular payments occur at a consistent time of night and identify who was in the building after hours.

Data Visualization Software

Data visualization helps to make complex data more understandable through visual depiction in terms of statistical graphics, plots, information graphics, tables, and charts. As the name suggests, these applications create powerful visualizations and highlight trends within structured data.

Effective Data Visualization

The following examples of data visualization demonstrate mock examples of the different ways that data can be brought to life to support different kinds of data analytics. Important numbers or analysis that might otherwise be buried in spreadsheets can be presented in charts, maps, and other graphics to identify spikes in activity, heightened risk, or business trends. Each dashboard provides a dynamic set of analyses that, when viewed comprehensively, may provide both internal auditors and managers greater visibility into high-risk activities, employees, or vendors.

Top 100 Riskiest Elements

Top 100 riskiest elements view identifies the top 100 riskiest third-party vendors, sorted from most risky to least risky. A risk ranking is generated for each third-party vendor by applying a set of rules to vendor information (location of work, transaction types, transaction amounts, vendor type, etc.). Each rule is scored and weighted and a final risk ranking is created for each third-party vendor. The histogram shows the distribution of mock third-party risk rankings across the entire vendor population (see **exhibit 14**).

Vendor Test Detailed Analysis

The vendor test detailed analysis view shows how a specific third-party vendor has performed on specific risk-ranking tests over time. This type of analysis is important when an organization's third-party vendor management policies and procedures are changed or if a specific vendor is working with the organization trying to improve (lower) their overall risk ranking. The trend line chart visually shows the total transaction spent by the third-party vendor on behalf of the organization and the average risk score associated with the spent amount (see **exhibit 15**).

Payments by Geography

The Corruption Perceptions Index[4] view is an example of using internal third-party vendor data as well as an external data source. The Corruption Perceptions Index rates each country on a scale of 0 (most risky) to 100 (least risky). The index data is used to match up countries where an organization's third-party vendors are doing business. The higher the corruption index of a country, the higher the risk of the third-party vendor transactions that are occurring within that country. This external data can then be overlaid with internal disbursement data to identify where payments are being made and assess the expectations around those payments (see **exhibit 16**).

Predictive Analytics

The actual and prediction transaction amounts view is used to predict future transaction amounts for an organization's third-party vendor. Based on historical data, a predictive transaction amount by month can be derived for any third-party vendor and then compared to actual transaction amounts that occurred. The bar graph is used to identify the widest gaps between actual amounts and predictive amounts. Wide gaps between actual and predictive are areas that are deemed high risk and would require investigation into the reason for the gaps (see **exhibit 17**).

Exhibit 14: Example of Third-Party Risk Rankings Across a Vendor Population

Top 100 Riskiest Elements

Test Type: FCPA Transaction Date: All Type: All

Transaction ID	Year of Transaction Date	Payee/EIN	Country/Dept	Type	Internal Approver	Trans Amount	Overall Test Average
23979	2012	ALSTOM HYDRO CHINA CO., LTD*97	Canada	Accountant	Shiflett	$191,908	75.75
10324	2010	ZOOMLION ZAMBIA LIMITED (REG. NO. 8..	Singapore	Accountant	Figlar	$84,878	75.00
22342	2013	BITTOHIN CHASI SOMAJ KALLYAN SANG..	Australia	Accountant	Mcleskey	$476,422	74.00
23708	2012	MR. TITH VOEURN*94	Saudi Arabia	Consultant	Bloes	$348,766	72.38
12189	2011	DIGIDATA	Norway	Other Professional Services	Grandstaff	$260,813	70.00
15400	2010	SURENDRA SINGH	Panama	Accountant	Muschett	$424,617	68.38
9779	2010	MR. SANJAY GUPTA*176	Gambia	Other Professional Services	Discher	$92,077	68.25
21423	2011	VLADIMIRO LOPEZ ROBLES	Netherlands	Accountant	Akhand	$243,633	68.25
16042	2012	MR. WIMPY IBRAHIM	Burundi	Accountant	Feeling	$10,675	68.00
306	2010	SNC-LAVALIN AIRPORT MANAAGEMENT ..	Suriname	Accountant	Nykiel	$240,834	67.88
8384	2013	LABH UNIVERSAL	Japan	Attorney	Kiltsch	$320,945	67.75
17494	2012	HAO ZHIYONG	Philippines	Accountant	Moodispaugh	$105,460	67.50
7942	2013	ARINC PERU S.A.C.	Seychelles	Consultant	Shealey	$320,524	66.88
3383	2010	SNC-LAVALIN TRANSPORTATION (AUST..	Estonia	Attorney	Giandelone	$402,840	65.50
18571	2012	PAVEL ZOLOTARYOV	India	Attorney	Fazzinga	$448,454	65.38
23611	2011	MR. MUNAWER KHALFAN*177	Singapore	Attorney	July	$268,236	64.63
6602	2011	SNC-LAVALIN TRANSPORTATION (AUST..	Somalia	Accountant	Demosthenes	$246,095	64.25
13378	2010	SLIVIA INC.*150	Kosovo	Joint Venture Partner	Fenoff	$102,703	62.63

Bin Size: 5

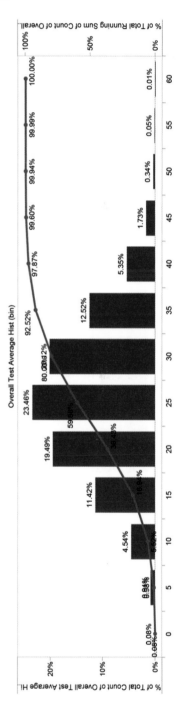

Source: Grant Thornton.

Exhibit 15: Example of a Third-Party Vendor Performance Over Time

Grant Thornton
An instinct for growth™

Vendor Test Detailed Analysis

Payee/EIN ZOOMLION ZAMBIA LIMITED (REG. NO. 88139) (AFFIL. ZOOMLION GHANA LTD.)*162

Test: Test 3 **Reason:** Multiple Values

Payee/EIN	Selected Reason	Year of Transa..	Avg. Selected Test	Number of Records	Trans Amount
ZOOMLION ZAMBIA LIMITED (REG. NO. 88139) (AFFIL. ZOOMLION GHANA LTD.)*162	Payment to Accountant - No Prior Relationship	2010	100.0	5	$754,295
		2011	100.0	3	$785,112
		2012	100.0	5	$1,500,643
		2013	100.0	2	$214,468
		Total	100.0	15	$3,254,518
	Payment to Attorney - No Prior Relationship	2010	75.0	2	$609,438
		2011	75.0	2	$796,952
		2012	75.0	3	$1,061,876
		2013	75.0	5	$808,571
		Total	75.0	12	$3,276,838
	Payment to Consultant - No Prior Relationship	2010	75.0	4	$603,206
		2011	75.0	1	$481,887
		2013	75.0	5	$1,750,938
		Total	75.0	10	$2,836,032
	Payment to Other Professional Services - No Prior Relationship	2010	50.0	2	$338,851
		2012	50.0	4	$1,204,758
		2013	50.0	4	$1,369,083
		Total	50.0	10	$2,912,692
Grand Total			77.7	47	$12,280,080

Source: Grant Thornton.

Exhibit 16: Corruption Perceptions Index

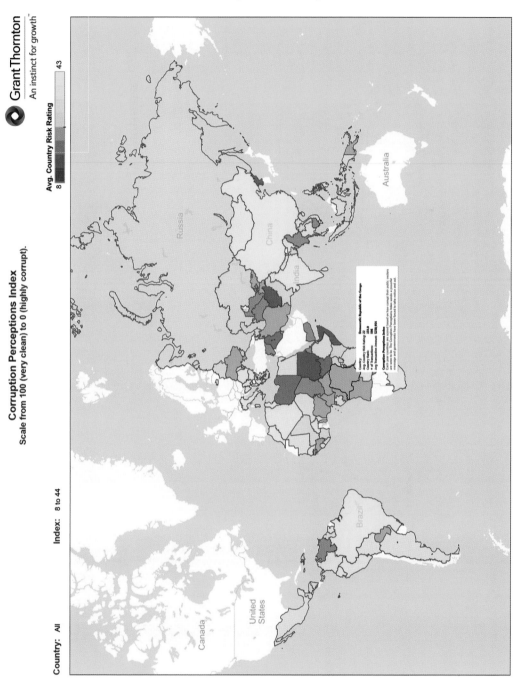

Source: Grant Thornton and Transparency International.

Exhibit 17: Example of Predictive Transaction Graphs

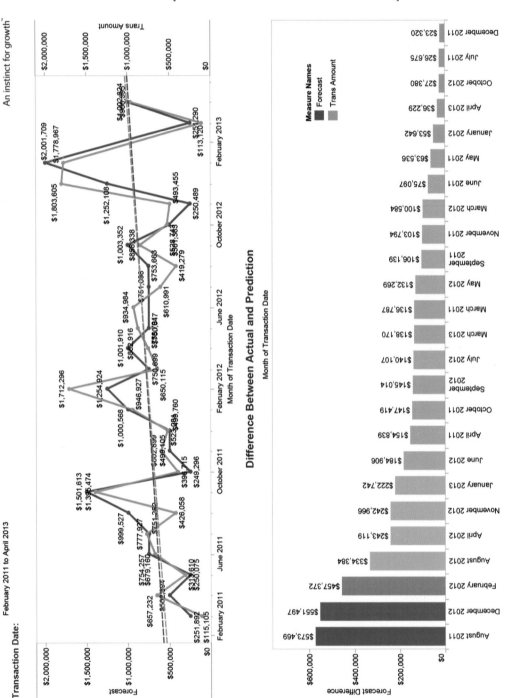

Source: Grant Thornton.

The research performed for this book supports the notion that directed analytics through data visualization is an area internal audit departments want to reach. Data visualization software is most useful in making comparisons, understanding causality, or presenting trending historical information that is not evident by simply viewing the data in its natural, structured form. Visualization tools are especially critical in presenting insights from data analytics in a way that the C-Suite and business unit leaders can quickly grasp, regardless of their experience with data. Based on the Data Analytics and Internal Audit Survey and interviews, Tableau is currently the most popular data visualization software used in internal audit.

Numerical Analysis Software

Numerical analysis software packages are powerful tools that require some degree of specialization and training to use. Typical analyses performed by this type of software include descriptive statistics (cross-tabulation, frequencies, and descriptive-ratio statistics), bivariate statistics (means, t-test, ANOVA, correlation, and nonparametric tests), prediction for numerical outcomes (linear regression), and prediction for identifying groups (factor analysis, cluster analysis, and discriminant analysis). Among today's tools, most do not have built-in, aesthetically pleasing visualization components, and secondary processing or data visualization software is required.

Numerical analysis tools are often used for statistical analysis in social science, as well as by market researchers, health-care researchers, survey companies, government entities, education researchers, and marketing organizations. For example, the Social Security Administration (SSA) compares actuarial lifespan data to ages of disability recipients to identify recipients who have lived beyond statistically anticipated lifespans for their ailments. This analysis enables SSA to identify anomalies and determine whether beneficiaries are deceased or cured of a disability, in which case they would be ineligible for payments. More recently, these tools have seen a larger presence in the accounting world, specifically in the realm of predictive analytics. With numerical analysis software, users can extract information from existing data sets to better determine patterns and predict future outcomes and trends.

Digital Forensic Tools

Digital forensic tools are valuable in the digital fraud arena, thanks to their ability to analyze unstructured data. These products analyze and interrogate images of electronic media such as computer hard drives, cellphones, external hard drives, servers, and other digital storage media. With digital forensic tools, users can perform deep dives into allocated and unallocated spaces on the acquired image, helping to analyze or recover deleted files, Internet activity, email correspondence, evidence linking to removable disks, computer log files/registries, and encrypted files.

These tools are used more often by special investigative teams rather than by internal audit. Just 1.1 percent of survey respondents reported they use EnCase, and less than 1 percent reported using FTK. Users of digital forensic tools often go through extensive training, which is typically accompanied by a certification for the particular software. An organization or internal audit department would likely have an investigative team or hire outside consultants to use these tools, although some larger companies might have the recurring need and resources to build an internal forensics team.

Executives increasingly expect internal audit to become a proactive partner and adviser to the business, but CAEs must first build the department's capabilities in three critical areas: people, process, and technology. Internal audit departments must first assemble or develop a team that can support implementation and rollout. To address data gaps, CAEs must be prepared to expand their influence across the organization while leading the charge in identifying those most applicable to their situation. Internal audit professionals must be prepared to illustrate how an expanded analytics budget and greater access to data will generate value.

IMPLEMENT, MONITOR, EVOLVE: A CONTINUOUS JOURNEY TO MATCH THE DATA ANALYTICS VISION WITH REALITY

Once CAEs have taken an inventory of their data analytics assets and the gaps they need to fill, they are ready for the final step in the Data Analytics Framework: translating the data analytics vision into action and impact. Research indicates that only about 30 percent of change initiatives are deemed successful,[1] so it is critical for CAEs to exhibit strong leadership in laying out the case for this new approach and seeing it through to completion. Ultimately, the CAE is responsible for ensuring that any investments in technology are matched by access to data and the talent needed to execute the analyses and extract insights from the results. For many CAEs, this more active role—equal parts data analytics ambassador, change agent, and strategic planner—may be uncharted territory. Indeed, clearly articulating a vision for internal audit involves rallying the department around this vision and selling it to the broader organization—from the C-Suite to the business unit leaders and frontline employees.

KEY TAKEAWAYS

» Managing a data analytics program should be an ongoing effort focused on enhancing capabilities in people, process, and technology.

» As an organization's needs change, the CAE should be prepared to adjust the road map accordingly.

» Management buy-in and support is a critical factor to ensure the program's long-term success.

» Case Study: Chevron

Obtaining buy-in from management begins during budget planning. CAEs must be forceful advocates for the investment in and expected returns from the implementation of data analytics capabilities. However, given internal audit's traditional role as a support function, they cannot lead this effort alone. They should rather look to align a coalition of business leaders and executives, including the chief information officer (CIO), who can speak to the impact that data analytics will have in the coming years and how investments in internal audit will benefit other departments and the broader organization as a whole. This leadership coalition should demonstrate and reinforce its belief that a comprehensive, well-planned data analytics effort is necessary to address a number of growing threats to the organization—from fraud to regulatory noncompliance, and even to cyber risks.

A successful implementation of data analytics within an internal audit function will require continual reinforcement. Once the initial proof of concept and implementation has been completed, CAEs must undertake critical self-evaluation on a regular basis, both to quantify the impact of current data analytics efforts and to identify procedural or technical enhancements. Because data analytics and its enabling technologies are evolving rapidly, CAEs must infuse their department with a mindset of continuous improvement to promote the sustained success of the investment.

Implement

Implementation of change is never as simple as flipping a switch. Much time and effort are required to coordinate people, process, and technology. The implementation should be addressed in stages, including differentiating between solution components.

People

Change is difficult. CAEs must identify and recruit (where necessary) resources that will champion the effort. In addition to identifying the right team, the organization should align individual performance evaluation goals with the broader goals of the data analytics initiative. Investments in training and professional development are also vital—CAEs must ensure that their team members either have the entire suite of skillsets in-house or can effectively collaborate with data analysts.

CAEs should also identify a resource to support the department day to day. Larger internal audit functions may hire a dedicated analyst, a luxury that often proves elusive for smaller departments. In such cases, and given the increasing need for data analytics in all facets of the organization, CAEs may be able to build a stronger business case for investment by collaborating with other department leaders. Demonstrating a consistent need for data analytics skillsets may provide the CAE with the justification to incorporate a dedicated internal audit resource into the budget.

Process

Enhancing the data analytics process begins with a focus on activities that are fundamental to data integrity, such as acquisition and cleansing. The internal audit team should continually assess the simple question, "How good is our data?" Even though advancements may be made in the automated acquisition and data quality assessment in the future, the continuous awareness and reassessment of data quality and integrity should become second nature to the internal audit function. This evolution will present CAEs with a choice of whether or not to invest in a new application or tool for this purpose. CAEs should consider the total cost of ownership in their decision-making process. For example, the investment (in terms of hours of staff time or dollars spent on new technologies) required to access certain data sets should be weighed in light of the potential benefits to current and future data analytics projects. In certain cases, investment in a new process may present opportunities to demonstrate long-term value, and additional data analytics resources to internal audit may become easier to justify.

The process improvement effort is not isolated to the internal audit function; rather, many business units responsible for data will need to collaborate around the common goal. As part of this outreach, internal audit leaders should aim to reinforce partnerships and identify the opportunities that data analytics presents toward achieving the organization's goals (e.g., revenue generation, cost reduction, and performance improvement). An emphasis on the mutual benefits of greater collaboration can help internal auditors shed the common misperception that they are mostly focused on identifying the errors and shortcomings of others.

Enhancement of the process is not isolated to considerations over data collection and storage. Internal audit should identify ways in which data analytics will improve the efficiency and effectiveness of the internal audit function. For example, it can use data analytics to enhance risk assessments by continuously targeting high-risk areas in a way that refines the scope during audit execution. This effort will include pinpointing audit areas that would benefit significantly from the application of data analytics to large volumes of data, as opposed to random or judgmental sampling. For certain procedures, such as the analysis of complex contracts that requires the review of supporting documentation, sampling will still be necessary. However, others, such as payment card processing, may benefit from analyzing the full population of data to identify trends, patterns, and, subsequently, anomalies. In still

> "Think of your existing power as the exponent in an equation that determines the value of information. The more power you have, the more additional power you derive from the new data."[3]
>
> —Bruce Schneier, American Cryptographer

other instances, data analytics might not enable internal audit to test 100 percent of all data sets, yet it increases audit assurance for minimal cost.[2]

For any proposed investments, CAEs must build a business case to identify the need and justify the request for resources. Determining a way to quantify the impact—by increased efficiency, expanded performance, or better strategic decision-making, for example—will contribute to a more effective pitch. In many cases, the actual outlay to purchase a new tool or system is comparatively small, so CAEs should focus on selling their comprehensive vision to the board and audit committee. It is important to manage expectations for the time frame of when investments will start to have an impact.

At an organizational level, internal audit frequently remains at the mercy of enterprise IT systems—both for the tools available to them and the ease of integrating new audit-specific applications. To take advantage of existing resources, internal audit should conduct an inventory of the technology platforms already in use by other departments. CAEs should work closely with their CIO counterpart to determine which solutions would be most effective in increasing access to data sources.

Monitor

Internal audit has a dual role in tracking the progress of its data analytics vision: self-assess the internal audit department's level of adoption and act as an independent party to facilitate improvement in other business units' use of data analytics. Creating a culture of data stewardship in which all players increase data access, quality, and consistency is a foundational element to the ongoing effort to integrate data analytics throughout the organization.

CAEs can take the following three steps to support this initiative and evaluate progress on a regular basis:

1. Select Metrics Along Each Category of the Maturity Model Framework

Select key performance indicators to evaluate the degree of the department's success. Basic questions to address include: Are the right people executing the data analytics vision? Can internal audit access the data sources required to support strategic priorities? Is the internal audit function using the proper tools (and functionality)?

2. Form a Data Analytics Governance/Review Team

To improve access to data and consistency around the process, a collaborative group consisting of the CAE, chief financial officer (CFO), chief operating officer (COO), CIO, internal audit team members, and other business line managers should be established to champion data analytics. By involving leaders from across the organization, the governance team should promote a culture of data excellence—a critical component of giving analysts high-quality data to work with.

3. Build On and Communicate Early Successes

CAEs should identify and promote instances where data analytics have been integrated into internal audit and have made a tangible positive initial impact on operations. By communicating these initial wins to business leaders, the CAE can build momentum for extending the application of data analytics to other operational areas. The Data Analytics and Internal Audit Survey found that most internal auditors are excited at the implementation of data analytics (see **exhibit 18**) and momentum will likely be supported from the bottom up.

Monitoring should be continuous and frequent. Internal audit should evaluate and monitor overall performance improvement to identify the impact data analytics has had on the organization. Certain evaluations, however, may occur infrequently due to the nature of the task. For example, low-risk audits may not be performed annually; it may take several years to gauge progress in certain areas.

Exhibit 18: Response to Data Analytics Integration

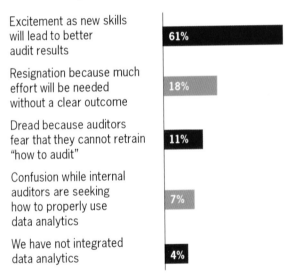

Source: The 2015 Data Analytics and Internal Audit Survey (The IIARF and Grant Thornton). Question 6: Which best describes the feeling of your internal audit department after integrating data analytics?

Beyond simply monitoring operations, CAEs should strive to be more involved in enterprise-wide processes touched by internal audit. This proactive approach requires understanding how the organization is changing and identifying new areas where data analytics can provide more transparency and insight. Along the Maturity Model Framework, internal audit functions should seek to build the capabilities to move from a more reactive, ad hoc approach to an agile and proactive mindset. By doing so, internal audit responds to risks quicker.

CASE STUDY:
HOW CHEVRON BUILDS ON ITS DATA ANALYTICS EFFORTS

A leader in the oil and gas industry, Chevron has more than 64,000 employees in its global operation. The corporate internal audit department is designed to not only help Chevron achieve its goals by providing objective assessments and recommendations on risk, internal controls, and governance, but also acts as a partner by providing stewardship and contributing to enterprise-wide talent development. One of the ways that corporate audit achieves these objectives is through data analytics.

While Chevron has incorporated data analytics into its audits for more than a decade, over the past three years, the department has developed and implemented close to 400 standardized reports that cover a variety of business processes. To support this effort, the company created a data resources team to provide data analytics support designed to assist in all phases of the audit. The initial implementation included the use of standardized analytics designed around the procurement, accounts payable, and vendor master processes. During each subsequent quarter, the company has increased its data analytics capabilities to cover additional areas, including contractors, user access, inventory, sales order management, fixed assets, and accounts receivables.

As a result of this standardization, Chevron has achieved the following benefits:

- Increased accuracy and consistency of execution during the audit phases (risk assessment, planning, and execution)
- Identification of potential risk areas during audit planning
- Efficiencies achieved through automated data extraction and repeatable audit tests
- Coverage of 100 percent of transactions
- Reductions in fieldwork

Once the audit teams began using the standardized reports, Chevron's business units started asking for access to run them themselves because it gave them data not easily available in the past. As a result, corporate audit has created a secure portal that enables the business units to download the same reports used by the internal audit teams, enabling the business units to enhance their monitoring controls and extending the functionality of the data analytics reports across the enterprise.

In addition to the standardized reports and the business unit access portal, the team has also developed and implemented several online tools to help with the administration of the data analytics reports. A feedback site captures comments and suggestions from each team and/or business unit that uses one of the standardized reporting packages. This allows for continuous learning and evolution and drives enterprise-wide support for not only the internal audit department but also the use of data analytics.

Evolve

A long-term vision and road map serve the critical purpose of setting a clear course for how to achieve defined objectives. The pace of technological advancements, a changing business environment, and an organization's growth can each alter the original calculus for the vision. The internal audit function should review and integrate new tools as they become available—something that is occurring in shorter and shorter intervals. Software will continue to be upgraded, adding more powerful features; enterprise systems will also enable improved access to data. Both developments can require adjustments to the data analytics vision.

As quickly as technology can change the equation, CAEs will also need to manage a much slower-evolving asset—their team members. In addition to investing in targeted training to get audit professionals more comfortable with data analytics, CAEs can seek to acquire additional human capital to fill any gaps. A promising internal audit data analyst candidate would have experience in data analytics, as well as some background in auditing and industry knowledge. MoneyGram Senior Vice President of Internal Audit Manny Rosenfeld noted, "The ideal data analytics resource will be highly logical and tech savvy, with an awareness of the business so they can come to us with ideas."

Another option to acquire the necessary skillset is to partner with established third-party vendors. Recognizing which tasks can be outsourced and what must be kept in-house is crucial for success in such an arrangement. Technology has also altered the equation considerably; internal audit procedures that previously needed to be performed onsite, such as bank confirmations and journal-entry testing, can now be outsourced to remote teams of specialists and third-party providers.[4] By tapping this flexible capacity, internal auditors employed by an enterprise can focus efforts on higher-risk areas such as fraud detection. Mary Ann Tourney, CAE of CF Industries, feels that while "internal audit can be co-sourced," data analysts should be members of the organization. The greater challenge is for internal audit to have consistent access to a data analyst. In addition, since many internal audit departments do not have the time or resources to keep up with analytics, third-party vendors can fill the gap while also deepening the team's understanding of data analytics.

More generally, CAEs should seek to build on successive waves of internal audit capabilities as they are developed. They should focus on iterative, small efforts built quickly by integrated teams. The ultimate goal should be to provide departments throughout the organization with the tools to gather, process, and analyze data regularly on their own (sometimes referred to as self-service analytics). For example, an internal audit could identify certain noncompliant transactions that lead to inappropriate revenue recognition or regulatory infractions. Based upon the attributes of the noncompliant transactions, the internal auditor can then design a routine report that produces exception reporting to identify these transactions routinely so that they can be corrected more timely. Once these reports are optimized, the internal auditor can then hand them over to the department to integrate into their respective business process.

Chapter 7

THE FUTURE OF DATA ANALYTICS IN INTERNAL AUDITING

Since the 1970s, Moore's Law has accurately predicted the evolution of computing power—in effect, that the number of transistors in a dense integrated circuit will double every two years. The impact of these advancements on data storage, management, and analysis has been transformative. Tasks that used to take a team of humans two years to accomplish can now be completed by algorithms in 20 minutes. While news stories often focus on the overwhelming quantity of data being generated, the future of business applications lies in *how* that data is being used.

As noted throughout this book, internal audit is generally behind the curve when it comes to the implementation of data analytics. Thanks to the integration of data analytics in the coming years, the internal audit department of the future will bear little resemblance to how most currently function. Imagine an organization as a virtual electronic footprint, growing rapidly in both size and complexity. Within internal audit, every professional will be conversant in data analytics; all enterprise data will be available, clean, and normalized; and data analytics will become the backbone of internal audit. Optimized audit schedules will enable internal audit to flag high-risk items automatically and give human users license to prioritize and investigate high-value areas. By letting computers handle the transactional, low-value tasks and engaging staff only on high-risk transactions that require human scrutiny, internal auditors will wield technology to achieve an unprecedented level of efficiency.

KEY TAKEAWAYS

» Over the next three to five years, internal audit departments will substantially enhance their data analytics capabilities.

» Powerful tools and new applications for data analytics will continue to emerge, so internal audit professionals must keep pace.

» Thanks to these technological advancements, internal audit's role and the composition of its team will change significantly.

» Case Studies: KeyBank and Cleveland Clinic

While gestural interfaces such as those featured in Steven Spielberg's 2002 film, *Minority Report,* are still a few years off, real-time data visualizations, driven by continuous monitoring of enterprise data, will become commonplace before the end of this decade. Analysis in the form of charts and graphs will be combined into interactive dashboards, allowing users to highlight and filter data to show relationships, correlations, and trends by the day, month, and year. Predictive analytics will be used to highlight vendors and employees with the "risk profile" to commit fraud, helping the internal audit function detect fraud and anomalies within the organization in real time and adjust processes and controls to prevent issues—sometimes before they even happen. As internal audit gains these capabilities, it will become an increasingly valued department thanks to its role in reducing corporate risk, driving operational improvement, and identifying impending changes in the business environment.

> "The big data revolution is that now we can do something with the data."[1]
>
> —Gary King, Director, Harvard's Institute of Quantitative Social Science

The 2015 Data Analytics and Internal Audit Survey reveals that internal audit professionals recognize that the future is here now, not a decade away. Nearly 90 percent of respondents believe their organization will place a greater emphasis on data analytics in the next three to five years (see **exhibit 19**).

Exhibit 19: Future Emphasis on Data Analytics

Do you believe there will be a greater emphasis on data analytics in your organization in the next 3-5 years?

● Yes
● No

Source: The 2015 Data Analytics and Internal Audit Survey (The IIARF and Grant Thornton). Question 7: Do you believe there will be a greater emphasis on data analytics in your organization in the next 3-5 years?

This time frame correlates with research, which suggests internal audit functions that are not yet on the journey toward implementing data analytics are already falling behind. "If you aren't adopting analytics or CAATs, you won't be effective," said Packaging Corporation of America's Mark Pearson. Mary Ann Tourney of CF Industries said, "All of my team members are embracing data analytics as the only way to audit in the future. There are so many changing elements in business. Manually finding the needle in the haystack is not going to work well."

In the coming years, the following capabilities will become standard elements of internal auditing.

Data-Enabled Insight

Continuous auditing and monitoring enable a steady, uninterrupted flow of data analysis, leading to the identification of high-risk elements in granular detail. These findings are stored in a relational database management system, and the data is presented through visualization tools to assist internal auditors in quickly identifying patterns, trends, and correlations that may otherwise go undetected. Properly designed data visualization dashboards can help internal audit and business staff make data-driven decisions instead of "gut" analysis on issues dealing with corporate risk. With this more accurate, near–real-time functionality, internal audit can play an increasingly important role in risk mitigation as well as operational issues.

Improved Resource Management

Automated continuous auditing will enable internal audit to cover more ground without adding employees. It can be used to perform many of the standard testing activities that in the past would be performed by internal audit staff. By allowing technology to perform many, if not all, of these routine tests, audit professionals can track and resolve critical high-risk transactions that have been identified through the automated processes.

Evidence-Based Predictions

The results of the continuous auditing and monitoring processes will be used as one key data source for predictive analytics. By combining audit and monitoring data along with historical data on vendors, employees, and transactions, internal audit can create profiles that identify a vendor or an employee with the propensity to perform specific activities that could result in, for example, an FCPA violation or expense fraud. Prescriptive analytics and mathematical algorithms will be used to select which vendors and employees should be audited, and the schedule for those audits will be optimized to maximize internal audit resources while minimizing costs.

Many CAEs are aware of these methods and features but have yet to implement them. According to the 2015 Global Internal Audit Common Body of Knowledge Practitioner Survey, continuous auditing is used extensively by just 14 percent of survey respondents—suggesting a high potential for explosive growth of its use across the industry.[2] The American Heart Association's Vickie Tesmer said, "With no barriers, the ideal tool is continuous auditing, where we get pinged when something comes up. We would develop it, the business unit could own it, and we could have more time to do other value-added tasks."

KeyBank is entering the next phase of its data analytics initiative by identifying the analytics that are candidates to be transferred to business units to support continuous monitoring. When making this determination, internal audit collaborated with business leaders to address the following factors:

- Automated solution that identifies high to moderately high findings specific to the line of business.

- The necessary data should be conducive to a repeatable process, with a low chance system migration.

- Value of analytics will be understood and recognized by the business unit (i.e., recovery of outstanding payments or alignment with enterprise initiatives).

KeyBank analyzes the following attributes of the data inputs when deciding if an analytic is a candidate for continuous monitoring: a) data availability; b) data comprehension; and c) data quality. Additionally, the analytic must address a significant risk, be repeatable and sustainable, and replace a manual process.

Technology on the Horizon

On an enterprise level, data analytics has already changed the way organizations operate. New categories of software and big data analysis will continue to revolutionize the field in the years ahead.

Machine Learning

The application of machine learning—the ability of a computer algorithm to learn and make predictions—will eventually replace many of the data analysis functions currently performed by humans. People exhibit a gradual learning curve. Machine learning will enable computers to accumulate knowledge and then quickly surpass the human ability to analyze data. As suggested in the introduction to this chapter, tasks that may take employees years can already be performed by machines in seconds. Examples are everywhere—from established text-recognition software to the current development of computerized photo recognition. Currently, humans are more adept at processing complex information, understanding relationships, and planning future actions—advantages that may erode as computers gain the ability to process data with a purpose, understand unstructured data, and use intuition.

For internal audit, computers will gradually take over more responsibility as they become more intelligent—especially in the realm of predictive analytics, anticipating risks, and alerting humans to potentially hazardous situations. To reap the huge rewards in efficiency, early detection, and accuracy, however, CAEs will need to ensure that their team's composition and internal audit's role continue to evolve as well.

Security Information Management

The Sony hacking scandal happened because someone with a legitimate user name and password went into systems that were highly unusual for that person's function. To address these types of security breaches, a new category of software called security information management (SIM) gathers security-related events (e.g., from end-user devices, servers, network equipment, and firewalls) in a centralized data storage location and allows near-real-time analysis. It tracks employee data strokes and activity both internally and externally in legacy systems, social media, and other interactions. The software uses statistical methods and rules to exclude false positives and identify employees doing potentially bad things. Every morning, the software produces a report that can support an investigation into the findings.

CASE STUDY:
CLEVELAND CLINIC—CAPTURING VALUE THROUGH DATA ANALYTICS

Don Sinko is the chief integrity officer of the Cleveland Clinic, a healthcare provider with a staff of 23 audit professionals for approximately 40,000 employees across the United States, Canada, and the United Arab Emirates. He oversees both the audit and compliance functions for one of the nation's top medical centers. Although these functions have different charters, their missions often merge, so the clinic uses a combination of both qualitative and quantitative steps to evaluate risk.

From the qualitative side, the organization reviews prior audit plans and identifies historical risks, interviews management to detect target areas, and tracks emerging trends through collaboration with industry peer groups. These qualitative steps are supported and augmented by data analytics on internal data, as well as the analytics performed by the U.S. Department of Health and Human Services (HHS). The department's Office of Inspector General publishes a yearly Work Plan that "summarizes new and ongoing reviews [with] respect to HHS programs and operations."[3] As the ultimate governing body for the nation's health insurance programs, HHS uses cutting-edge methodologies and software to collect and mine data from multiple sources and identify trends and benchmarks.[4] Because the results of these analytics are already available (and identified as target areas by the government), Cleveland Clinic mirrors the target areas that are applicable to its businesses to identify exposures and any opportunities to enhance compliance.

In addition to these predefined tests, Cleveland Clinic performs a suite of analytics around financial, operational, and medical risks. The possibility of a Health Insurance Portability and Accountability Act (HIPAA) breach is one of the top concerns for Sinko (and Cleveland Clinic's information security team). To mitigate this specific cyber risk, the clinic applies emerging data analytics solutions that provide real-time monitoring and alerting based on threat level, including the average time and total medical records reviewed by clerical staff, and when users are spending an inordinate amount of time and activity (captured by the amount of clicks) in systems. The clinic also uses a data-in-motion tool that examines emails and alerts containing patient information.

As with every organization, Cleveland Clinic has limited funds to accomplish its mission, which is to advance medical innovations and provide better, faster, cheaper care for patients. For internal audit, this organizational focus means that investments are typically compliance-driven and do not result in revenue windfalls. However, Sinko was able to secure funding for staffing and technology around cybersecurity by making it a priority and mapping the potential tangible costs of a HIPAA breach. This exercise created a new term to quantify value for internal audit: return on compliance (ROC).

The Internet of Things

Beyond the aforementioned exploding volume of data, the Internet of Things (IoT)—the ability of any device to connect to the Internet, communicate with other devices, and generate data—holds immense promise. While executives and technologists continue to speculate on how organizations can harness this data, few dispute that the IoT will transform the business world and daily life. For internal audit, the potential of a multitude of devices churning out unstructured data has yet to be defined. The availability of more data also leads to additional exposure for the organization (i.e., cyber risks) that must be managed to determine the appropriate risk appetite.

These three examples have huge implications for the enterprise and for internal audit. Functions (and entire companies) that are just getting started down the path of the Data Analytics Framework may need to build capabilities and expertise before embarking on such large-scale projects. However, internal audit can position itself as an active partner in these efforts by starting the conversation, defining a use case, and creating connections with other departments.

An Expanded Role for Internal Audit

Today's changing environment has set internal audit on a path where data analytics will be critical to any high-performing function. The board increasingly expects the CAE to not only lead internal audit but also drive efforts, reduce risk, detect fraud, contribute to regulatory compliance, and support operational improvement. As discussed in chapter 4, fulfilling this expanded role will require the CAE to create closer connections to other business units. For example, to drive operational improvement, internal audit will need to identify risks and work closely with legal to mitigate those risks (for example, by terminating contracts with certain vendors).

The charter for internal audit is expanding quickly. CAEs must embrace the opportunity to raise their profile in the organization, enhance the capabilities of internal audit, and take concrete steps to unlock the full potential of data analytics. Whether they need cooperation, resources, or both, it is up to the CAE to build the business case.

"IoT is changing and transforming everything from business to life. Imaginations are boundless and opportunities are infinite. Everything is being wired up or connected wirelessly—architecture, energy-efficient sensing, secure networks, quality of service, new protocols, participatory sensing, data mining, GIS-based visualization, cloud computing, and international activities. It simply means that powerful information will be at our fingertips."[5]

—Mehul Nayak,
Digital Marketing
Consultant

CONCLUSION

Implementing data analytics into internal audit is no longer a question of *when* but *how*. Organizations in all industries and of all sizes recognize the need for data analytics and are actively searching for tangible advice as they take this journey. By using examples of how world-class organizations have implemented data analytics into their function, the challenges faced, and the key elements of a successful program, a Data Analytics Framework was formed.

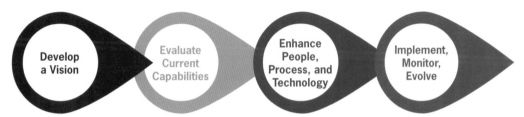

Setting a strategic vision for how data analytics enables internal audit's mission allows the department to recognize gaps in its current capabilities. Enhancing the data analytics skills of people through a structured process will allow technology to enable and expedite the approach. Finally, implementing the framework requires monitoring and subsequent mapping back to the intended vision to identify how the program (or the vision) must evolve.

There is no one-size-fits-all approach to integrating data analytics into their operations. However, organizations that are successful are achieving greater clarity and assurance by augmenting sampling with data analytics to review 100 percent of the data at a relatively small cost. They are investing in new software and tools that can increase efficiency. They are getting buy-in from the C-Suite and board. And they are starting to reap the benefits of these efforts in the form of a more active role. If information is power, then internal audit departments will be well-positioned to have a greater impact on the organization.

> "The price of light is less than the cost of darkness."[1]
>
> —Arthur Nielsen, American Market Analyst

Observers will look back on these years as a period of transition. Internal auditors today are just beginning to understand the myriad ways that data analytics can support the function. By contrast, the next generation of internal audit professionals has grown up in a digital world, where technology and devices are ever-present and constant change is an enabler rather than an obstacle. As this crop of leaders takes the helm, the evolution of internal auditing will accelerate and data analytics will be integrated into every facet of the profession. The result will be an era of unprecedented efficiency, transparency, and assurance.

Whether an internal audit department is at the vanguard of data analytics or has yet to engage, it is not too late. With the fundamentals in place and strategic investment in the right capabilities, internal audit departments can unlock the full potential of data analytics. Seizing this opportunity now—let alone in the future—requires leaders to immediately begin formulating a vision for data analytics.

Appendix A

SOFTWARE TOOLS

Below is an inventory of software tools that may be used for data analytics. The list was prepared based on information that is publicly available and is not intended to be an exhaustive list of software tools that are available. Please visit each vendor website to gain a better understanding of each product's capabilities.

Software Solution	Website for Additional Information
ACL (Audit Command Language)	http://www.acl.com
Alteryx	http://www.alteryx.com
CaseWare IDEA	http://www.audimation.com
ClickView	http://www.qlik.com
EMC	http://www.emc.com
Gephi	http://gephi.github.io
IBM Cognos	http://www.ibm.com
IBM SPSS	http://www.ibm.com
Microsoft SQL Server	http://www.microsoft.com
My SQL	https://www.mysql.com
Oracle Data Mining	http://www.oracle.com
Oracle Data Visualization	https://cloud.oracle.com
Oracle RDMS	http://www.oracle.com
Pure Storage	https://www.purestorage.com
Revolution Analytics (R)	http://www.revolutionanalytics.com
RiverLogic	http://www.riverlogic.com
SAS	http://www.sas.com
SAS Visual Analytics	http://www.sas.com
Spotfire	http://spotfire.tibco.com
Tableau	http://www.tableau.com

NOTES

Chapter 1
What Does Data Analytics Mean to Internal Audit?

1. Quote by Peter Sondergaard, senior vice president, Gartner Research.

2. AICPA, "Audit Analytics and Continuous Audit," p. 92, https://www
   .aicpa.org/InterestAreas/FRC/AssuranceAdvisoryServices/Pages/
   ContinuousAssuranceWorkingGroup.aspx.

3. "Chinese cave 'graffiti' tells a 500-year story of climate change and impact
   on society," *Science Daily,* August 13, 2015, http://www.sciencedaily.com/
   releases/2015/08/150813092816.htm.

4. Quote by Rutherford D. Rogers, American librarian, chief of personnel at the
   New York Public Library, chief of the reference department, deputy librarian
   of Congress, director of libraries, Stanford University, and university
   librarian, Yale University.

5. "What is Big Data?" http://www.ibm.com.

6. "Big Data, Bigger Digital Shadows, and Biggest Growth in the Far East,"
   IDC Digital Universe study, February 2013, https://www.emc.com/collateral/
   analyst-reports/idc-digital-universe-united-states.pdf.

7. Quote by Nate Silver, American statistician and writer who analyzes baseball
   and elections. He is currently the editor-in-chief of ESPN's FiveThirtyEight
   blog and a special correspondent for ABC News.

8. Structured Versus Unstructured Data: The Balance of Power Continues to
   Shift, International Data Corporation, March 2014, http://www.idc.com.

9. For more detail, see Karen A. Frenkel, "12 steps for analyzing unstructured
   data," *CIO Insight*, February 2, 2015, http://www.cioinsight.com/it-strategy/
   big-data/slideshows/12-steps-for-analyzing-unstructured-data.html.

10. Quote by Alvin Toffler, American writer and futurist, known for his
    works discussing the digital revolution, communication revolution, and
    technological singularity. Toffler is a former associate editor of *Fortune*
    magazine.

11. Quote by Ronald Harry Coase, British economist and author. For much of
    his life, he was the Clifton R. Musser Professor Emeritus of Economics at the
    University of Chicago Law School, where he arrived in 1964 and remained
    for the rest of his life.

12. "The value of analytics in healthcare," IBM Global Business Services, IBM Institute for Value, 2012.

13. "Ten ways big data is revolutionizing manufacturing," *Forbes Tech*, 2014.

14. "How big data can improve manufacturing," McKinsey & Company, 2014, http://www.mckinsey.com/insights/operations/how_big_data_can_improve _manufacturing.

15. Anthony Hernandez and Kevin Morgan, "Prescriptive analytics: Winning in a competitive environment," http://www.grantthornton.com/issues/library/ whitepapers/advisory/2014/BAS-prescriptive-analytics.aspx.

16. Walker, Tracey, "Just 10% of healthcare organizations using data analytics," *Managed Healthcare Executive*, April 30, 2015, http:// managedhealthcareexecutive.modernmedicine.com/managed-healthcare -executive/news/just-10-healthcare-organizations-using-data-analytics.

Chapter 3
Develop a Vision: Understanding How Data
Analytics Will Support Internal Audit

1. Quote by Jeff Weiner, CEO of LinkedIn, a business-related social networking website.

2. Larry Harrington, *Driving Success in a Changing World: 10 Imperatives for Internal Audit* (Altamonte Springs, FL: The Institute of Internal Auditors Research Foundation), p. 9.

3. *Adding internal audit value: Strategically leveraging compliance activities*, Grant Thornton, 2014.

4. Ken Tysiac, "10 imperatives for internal audit," *Journal of Accountancy*, July 7, 2015.

5. John Jordan, "The Risks of Big Data for Companies," *The Wall Street Journal*, October 20, 2013, http://www.wsj.com/articles/ SB10001424052702304526204579102941708296708.

6. Paul Byrnes et al., *Reimagining Auditing in a Wired World*, AICPA, August 2014, https://www.aicpa.org/interestareas/frc/assuranceadvisoryservices/ downloadabledocuments/whitepaper_blue_sky_scenario-pinkbook.pdf.

7. *Audit Analytics and Continuous Audit*, AICPA, 2015, p. 107.

8. Benford's Law offers a method for data analysis based on the observation that in some (but not all) data sets, certain numbers appear more frequently. For more information, see Durtschi et al., "The Effective Use of Benford's Law to Assist in Detecting Fraud in Accounting Data," *The Journal of Forensic Accounting*, 1524–5586, vol. V (2004), pp. 17–34, https://www.agacgfm.org/ AGA/FraudToolkit/documents/BenfordsLaw.pdf.

Chapter 4
Evaluate Current Capabilities: Performing a Data Analytics Self-Diagnostic

1. *Audit analytics and continuous audit*, AICPA, 2015.

2. IIA Position Paper, The Three Lines of Defense in Effective Risk Management and Control (Altamonte Springs, FL: The Institute of Internal Auditors), January 2013.

3. Quote by David McCandless, British data journalist and information designer based in London. He is the founder of the visual blog, "Information is Beautiful."

Chapter 5
Enhance People, Process, and Technology: The Key Ingredients to Data Analytics Implementation

1. The 2015 Data Analytics and Internal Audit Survey did not include these questions.

2. Michael P. Cangemi, *Staying a Step Ahead: Internal Audit's Use of Technology* (Altamonte Springs, FL: The Institute of Internal Auditors Research Foundation), p. 7.

3. *GTAG 16: Digital Analysis Technologies*, Global Technology Audit Guide (Altamonte Springs, FL: The Institute of Internal Auditors), 2011.

4. Corruption Perceptions Index, Transparency International, http://www .transparency.org/.

Chapter 6
Implement, Monitor, Evolve: A Continuous Journey to Match the Data Analytics Vision with Reality

1. "3 success factors for transformational change," Grant Thornton, 2015.

2. *Audit Analytics and Continuous Audit: Looking Toward the Future* (New York, NY: American Institute of Certified Public Accountants, Inc.), 2015.

3. Quote by Bruce Schneier, American cryptographer, computer security and privacy specialist, and writer. He is the author of several books on general security topics, computer security, and cryptography.

4. Maria Murphy and Ken Tysiac, "Data analytics helps auditors gain deep insight," *Journal of Accountancy*, April 13, 2015.

Chapter 7
The Future of Data Analytics in Internal Auditing

1. Jonathan Shaw, "Why 'Big Data' is a Big Deal," *Harvard Magazine*, March–April 2014, http://harvardmagazine.com/2014/03/why-big-data-is-a-big-deal.

2.   Michael P. Cangemi, *Staying a Step Ahead: Internal Audit's Use of Technology* (Altamonte Springs, FL: The Institute of Internal Auditors Research Foundation), p. 7.

3.   See the 2016 Work Plan at http://oig.hhs.gov/reports-and-publications/workplan/index.asp#current.

4.   For example, the 2016 Work Plan's "Prescription Drugs—Billings and Payments" section noted that "payments for immunosuppressive drug claims with KX modifiers" will receive additional scrutiny.

5.   Quote by Mehul Nayak, digital marketing consultant at Softweb Solutions and Softweb IoT, an IoT solutions provider company based in Chicago. He is responsible for enhancing brand awareness and increasing the visibility of a company's products and services.

Conclusion

1.   Quote by Arthur Charles Nielsen, American market analyst and founder of the global market research firm AC Nielsen Company.

Key Terminology

Chief Audit Executive – A person in a senior position responsible for effectively managing the internal audit activity in accordance with the internal audit charter and The IIA's Definition of Internal Auditing, the Code of Ethics, and the *International Standards for the Professional Practice of Internal Auditing (Standards)*.

Compliance – Adherence to policies, plans, procedures, laws, regulations, contracts, or other requirements.

Computer-Assisted Audit Techniques (CAATs) – CAATs have a wide range of uses within internal audit, investigations, management accounting, and general inquiries. These software tools analyze data to highlight potentially fraudulent transactions, compliance issues, and internal control weaknesses.

Continuous Auditing – The automated performance of an audit activity on a regularly repeated basis that gives timely insight into an organization's risk and control issues.

Continuous Monitoring – The automated review of business processes and controls. It helps an organization detect errors, fraud, abuse, and system inefficiencies.

Data Analytics – The science of examining raw data to draw conclusions about that information. Internal audit professionals use it for compliance, fraud detection and investigation, operational performance, and internal controls assessment.

Data Analytics Framework – The framework consists of four steps: 1) develop a vision, 2) evaluate current capabilities, 3) enhance people, process, and technology, and 4) implement, monitor, and evolve.

Data Analytics Software – Tools that help complete data analysis. See appendix A.

Data Visualization – Helps to make complex data more understandable through visual depiction in terms of statistical graphics, plots, information graphics, tables, and charts.

Descriptive Analytics – The reporting of past events to characterize what has happened. It condenses large chunks of data into smaller, more meaningful bits of information.

Diagnostic Analytics – Provides insight into why certain trends or specific incidents occurred. Enables analysts to gain a better understanding of business performance, market dynamics, and how different inputs affect the outcome.

Internal Audit Activity – A department, division, team of consultants, or other practitioner(s) that provides independent, objective assurance and consulting services.

Maturity Model Framework – A proprietary diagnostic tool that outlines five progressive stages for internal audit departments: 1) ad hoc, 2) defined, 3) repeatable, 4) institutionalized, and 5) optimized.

Operational Performance – Defined as an organization's performance measured against a standard or prescribed indicators of effectiveness, efficiency, and environmental responsibility.

People, Process, and Technology – People (the ability of internal audit team members to embrace data analytics); process (the method an organization uses to access data and integrate it into its daily tasks); and technology (the platforms, systems, and tools that enable data analytics).

Predictive Analytics – Allows users to extract information from large volumes of existing data, apply certain assumptions, and draw correlations to predict future outcomes and trends.

Prescriptive Analytics – Requires a significant volume of data to first make predictions and then link them to actions that will produce the best result.

Risk Mitigation – Defined as a systematic reduction in the extent of exposure to a risk and/or the likelihood of its occurrence.

THE IIA RESEARCH FOUNDATION
SPONSOR RECOGNITION

STRATEGIC PARTNER

PRINCIPAL PARTNERS

EY
Building a better
working world

PRESIDENT'S CIRCLE (US $25,000+)

CHAIRMAN'S CIRCLE (US $15,000–$24,999)

FOUNDATION PARTNERS (US $5,000–$14,999)

Erich Schumann, CIA, CRMA

Raytheon

Larry Harrington, CIA, CRMA, QIAL